Adrien Sylvain, Ella McMahon

Golden Sands

A Collection of Little Counsels for the Sanctification and Happiness of Daily Life

Adrien Sylvain, Ella McMahon

Golden Sands

A Collection of Little Counsels for the Sanctification and Happiness of Daily Life

ISBN/EAN: 9783337417765

Printed in Europe, USA, Canada, Australia, Japan

Cover: Foto ©Lupo / pixelio.de

More available books at **www.hansebooks.com**

A COLLECTION

OF

LITTLE COUNSELS

FOR THE

SANCTIFICATION AND HAPPINESS OF DAILY LIFE.

Translated from the French.

BY MISS ELLA McMAHON.

THIRD SERIES.

NEW YORK, CINCINNATI AND CHICAGO:
BENZIGER BROTHERS,
Printers to the Holy Apostolic See.

We heartily approve and commend the excellent little work entitled "Golden Sands," translated into English from the original French. We hope it will receive a welcome in every household.

John Card. McCloskey
Archbp. of New York

APPROBATIONS.

Upon the very favorable report of our committee we approve of this volume, of the interesting collection entitled *Golden Sands*, as we did of the preceding series, and we recommend it to lovers of good reading.

✠ LOUIS, *Archbishop of Avignon.*

AVIGNON, September 17, 1879.

The book itself is beyond praise, and will assuredly be of great spiritual benefit to those who read it carefully. It is appropriately named, since it contains so many pious and truly beautiful thoughts. I hope it will meet with a ready sale.

✠ W. M. WIGGER,
Bishop of Newark.

NEWARK, October 11, 1882.

TABLE OF CONTENTS.

CHAPTER		PAGE
I.	My Crucifix	13
II.	The Bird Charmer	14
III.	The Way to God	17
IV.	They know I love them, why should I tell them so?	20
V.	A little recipe for the use of persons destined to live together	21
VI.	Amen—Alleluia!	23
VII.	Little devices for restoring peace to the soul, and causing it to acquire merits	28
VIII.	Simple counsels to a young girl	37
IX.	Recipes for never wearying friends	38
X.	Before God, before God alone	41
XI.	How the Saints know how to love	45
XII.	Little devices for restoring peace to the soul, and causing it to acquire merit	46
XIII.	Simple counsels to young girls	50
XIV.	Sanctification	56
XV.	Little devices to restore peace to the soul, and to cause it to acquire merit	60
XVI.	Prayer of a Christian soul	64
XVII.	The soul's thirst	65
XVIII.	How souls are cured	70
XIX.	A few thoughts upon the confession of pious persons	76
XX.	Have you your photograph?	81
XXI.	The gate of Heaven is very narrow	86

Contents.

CHAPTER		PAGE
XXII.	Memorial for the Children of Mary	87
XXIII.	The demons of the hearth	91
XXIV.	Little devices for restoring peace to the soul, and causing it to acquire merit	95
XXV.	The *fiat* of a desolate soul	99
XXVI.	Apostleship in a family.	101
XXVII.	The Samaritan's balm	103
XXVIII.	Provisions of the soul	105
XXIX.	To make friends	109
XXX.	Little devices for restoring peace to the soul, and causing it to acquire merit	115
XXXI.	The Holy Shadow	120
XXXII.	Useless	124
XXXIII.	What the smile of a Saint says	126
XXXIV.	The power of an Act of Love of God	130
XXXV.	Wings	134
XXXVI.	Be serious	139
XXXVII.	A Child of Mary's life. What a Child of Mary should be	140
XXXVIII.	An unknown joy	145
XXXIX.	Consolation	148
XL.	A charming means of being kind and securing happiness	150
XLI.	The Communion which sanctifies the soul	155
XLII.	A flattery inspired by the heart	161
XLIII.	A few moments before an image of the Blessed Virgin	162
XLIV.	How God brings back souls	176
XLV.	The Abbé Pereyve	180
XLVI.	That which could make me unhappy	180
XLVII.	The song of the conscience	186
XLVIII.	Litany of goodness and devotion	191

GOLDEN SANDS.

In the summer, in the South of France, little children and the infirm poor, incapable of hard labor, in order to earn a little bread, occupy themselves in collecting from the beds of half-dried rivers *golden sands* which are carried by the water in its course and glisten in the sun.

What these poor and little ones do with the *golden sands* which God has scattered in these unknown rivers, let us attempt, with these little *counsels* which God has scattered everywhere to sparkle, and glisten, and comfort for an instant, then to disappear, leaving to the soul the regret of not having gathered them.

Who has not sometimes felt the strength of some sweet and simple *les-

son which thrilled him, and revealed to him suddenly a world of peace, of devotion, and of joy?

It was a *word* read in a book, a *remark* heard by accident in conversation, but which had for us a particular meaning, and left us with an unknown strength. It was a *smile* surprised on the lips of one whom we loved, and yet knew to be suffering, which told us of the joy of resignation. It was the *frank look* of an innocent child which revealed to us all the sweetness and gentleness of simplicity.

Oh! if we knew how to gather and fix in our souls these lessons which gleam for *an instant* like a luminous ray, how useful they would be to us in days of discouragement and sorrow.

What wise counsels we would find in them for our conduct!

What consolation for our aching hearts!

What ingenious means of doing good!

It is this simple work of *collecting* a little everywhere, from *nature*, from *books*, from *souls* particularly, that one of your brothers proposes to do for you, dear friends, who desire to lead holy and devout lives.

And as these little *sands of gold* which are singly gathered from the bed of the stream bring, when collected, each month a little comfort to homes of the poor, so he wishes to bring each month a little joy to your heart and a little peace to your souls.

Welcome these little leaves, which have all been written under the maternal auspices of the Blessed Virgin; welcome them with kindness. Let them penetrate a moment to your soul, then scatter them, that they may bear their good words to others.

They will not be importunate, they will not even ask to be preserved; what matters life to them, if they do *good in passing?*

GOLDEN SANDS.

WE come once more, the little *Golden Sands*, to take at your fireside the corner you have reserved for us during the past nine years.

A very modest, retired little corner, where we shall always remain, attracting little attention, waiting in the presence of God, until you ask of us a word of *counsel*, a word of *encouragement*, a word of *cheer*.

In a book written by one of those superior minds whom all who try to write regard as their master, we find these words, which we ask his permission to make our own:

"I wish—I have not yet attained my desire, but I hope to reach it—I wish I might be the tree which throws a little shade on the dusty roadside; the gentle breeze which refreshes the plain; the perfume of the hidden flower; the song of the bird which cheer the heart of the wayfarer.

"Passing brother, I love thee and I ask nothing in return. Accept the shade of the tree, the freshness of the breeze, the perfume of the flower, the song of the bird. God gives them to thee, take them, go on thy way with thy happiness and thank only God."

This is the desire of *Golden Sands* beginning their tenth year.

Pius IX., speaking of a few pious leaflets, for which we asked a benediction, said, "*I love these little messengers of God; one alone sometimes does more for me than a missionary.*"

Our little leaflets are read at Rome. Archbishops, Cardinals, have deigned to approve the Italian and English translations. Oh, that an angel might bear them to Pius IX., and our beloved Holy Father, receiving them with affection, could say, "*I love these little messengers of the good God!*"

When in the month of January, 1877, we expressed the desire to have our *Golden Sands* reach Pius IX., we did not think that a few months afterwards the Sovereign Pontiff to whom a pious hand had offered our humble little leaves would deign to smile upon them and encourage us to continue their publication.

The *Brief* which we received is too honorable not to insert here. It shall be for our collection like those drops of balm which we pour upon frail and delicate plants to preserve them indefinitely, and to increase their perfume.

BRIEF

Addressed in the name of His Holiness Pius IX.

To the Author

AND

To the Publishers of Golden Sands

His Holiness, our Holy Father Pius IX., was happy to receive the volume containing the pious readings published from the year 1868 to the year 1876, under the title of *Golden Sands*, which you sent him with your letter as proof of your devotion and respectful affection.

His Holiness is happy to congratulate you on your zeal in writing and propagating these leaflets, the object of which, as their title indicates, is the sanctification of souls, and he does not doubt that, approved and recommended as they are by several bishops, as you cause him to remark, they will greatly contribute to the spiritual profit of those who may read them.

His Holiness accepts with fatherly kindness the sentiments of filial love expressed in your letter, and wishes you an abundance of all heavenly graces, and, as presage of these graces, sends you the apostolic blessing which you ask.

CHARLES NOCELLA,
Latin Secretary to His Holiness.
ROME, April 14, 1877.

Golden Sands.

I.

MY CRUCIFIX.

It was in a modest cell at the foot of a crucifix that we read these pious lines which we are about to transcribe.

"Copy them, propagate them, above all love them," said the religious, from whom we asked them, "and when your heart is crushed by one of those sorrows more torturing in the world than in our quiet retreat, when your soul is prostrated by neglect, abandonment and fear, kneel before your crucifix, and affectionately kissing the feet of the Divine Consoler, slowly repeat these words.

"Oh, how many tears they have dried!

"But if you heed me you will keep

them for a time of sorrow and trial, at other times you may not understand them.

MY CRUCIFIX.

I bear it everywhere, I prefer it to all things!
My Crucifix.

When I fall, it raises me;
When I weep. it consoles me;
When I suffer, it cures me;
When I tremble, it reassures me;
When I call, it answers me.
My Crucifix.

It is the light which enlightens me,
The sun which warms me,
The food which nourishes me,
The fountain which refreshes me,
The sweetness which inebriates me,
The balm which heals me,
The beauty which charms me.
My Crucifix.

It is the solitude where I repose,
The fortress wherein I am enclosed,
The furnace where I am consumed,
The ocean wherein I am submerged.
The abyss wherein I am plunged.
My Crucifix.

I wish to desire nothing but thee!
To seek but thee!
To ask but thee!
To love but thee!
To keep but thee!
   MY CRUCIFIX.

Sustain me during labor,
Guard me during life,
Reassure me in my agony,
Be upon my heart in my last hour,
   O MY CRUCIFIX.

II.

THE BIRD CHARMER.

He was an old man with a gentle kind face, a calm expression and a restful smile.

Little birds flew about him flapping their wings and giving little joyous chirps.

They came and went, lighting upon the old man's head, then upon his shoulder, or upon the ground at his feet to take the crumbs he was scattering for them; others bolder than the rest lit upon his hand and fed from his fingers.

And you could see that the good old man was happy in their confidence, happier still perhaps to do good.

A child, marvelling at the tameness of the birds, said to her mother,

"But what does he give them to attract them?"

"Only bread."

"Bread! Oh, I'll give them cake; how they will flock about me!"

And drawing quite near the charmer the child began to scatter crumbs of cake, beckoning to the birds and calling, "birdie, little birdie!"

The timid birds took flight.

The disappointed little one followed them with her eyes, murmuring, "*Yet I gave them cake.*"

"My child," the old man said gently, "to win birds, to win hearts to us, it is not sufficient to *give them good things, we must give in a way which will please them.*"

Is not this a lesson for us at the beginning of a new year of *Golden Sands?*

It is not merely for diversion nor even for the sweet and at the same time allowable pleasure of finding them looked for and welcomed that we publish these *little leaves.* We have a mission to fulfil, and, to fulfil this mission, O that we were *charmers to attract hearts, to attract souls, that we might bring them to Thee, my God!*

III.

THE WAY TO GOD.

A few days before *New Years*, at the house of a friend, I saw a magnificently bound volume on a table little accustomed to such luxurious objects.

"For whom is this expensive present?" I asked in astonishment.

"For little Lucy."

"What! for a child ten years old!"

"Why of course *it is not for her, but*

for her parents. The child receives it, but it is to the father I give it."

_

Does not God wish by these simple words to convey a light, an inspiration, to my soul?

In a family the child is the surest and most direct way to the father's heart.

When we wish to *ask* a favor, and hesitate to make a direct offering for fear of wounding, we place it in the hands of the child, and the *father's heart* is moved to benevolence.

If we wish to make some return for a favor, and, finding no offering worthy of the benefactor, we give a present to the child; it goes to the *father's heart*, and the benefactor becomes the debtor.

We wish to *give pleasure*, and, not knowing how to proceed, we again place an offering in the hands of the child, and rejoice the *father's heart*.

***

Ah my God! are not all who surround me *Thy children, Thy beloved children*, even though they weary me, try me, or annoy me?

Is he not Thy child, this poor man who holds out his hand to me in the street; this *servant* who waits upon me; this relative with whom I am obliged to live; this companion in labor who tries me and wearies me?

Do the rags which cover bodies, the difficult temper, ill will, which envelop souls, prevent Thee from loving them and *being present to see each moment what I do for them?*

***

If, then, I have a grace to ask of God, a thanksgiving to render Him, what I must do to be heard or accepted is to make a *present* to one of His children.

And I do not need to go far, nor to seek a very expensive gift. I have not to concern myself whether my gift will be appreciated by *the child;* I am sure that my *generosity* will be appreciated by the *father.*

This child of God, the most beloved child of God, is at present the person who is nearest to me.

This present which I can make is a *word of encouragement, a mark of affection, interesting news, labor performed for our neighbor, an encouraging smile, a prayer for a soul, a kind thought.*

* *
*

Ah, when you shall have done *something* for one of God's children go without fear and bear your request, your thanksgiving to Jesus Christ; you will be always welcomed.

The surest and most direct way to the heart of a father is through the heart of his child.

IV.

We easily thank those to whom we are more or less *indifferent,* but we are so accustomed to think that those we love must read our thoughts and know our gratitude, that they are the ones we thank least *in words.*

And yet is it not particularly to you poor loved ones that we should express our affection and gratitude?

"*They know that I love them*, why should I tell *them so?* Why? To give them pleasure, to show them that we appreciate what they do for us.

Oh, then let us who love each other utter more frequently *those sweet words of friendship*, which are to the heart what dew is to the plant.

V.

A LITTLE RECIPE FOR THE USE OF PER-SONS DESTINED TO LIVE TOGETHER.

I.

"You love each other, do you not?"
"Yes, but—"
"But— what?"

"Oh, *he* has a good, a very good heart, but if you knew what a trying disposition! For three years now I have struggled and prayed and scolded, but alas—"

"Three years! if for three years you had tried my *recipe*, you would no longer feel the asperities of his disposition, you would not even suspect that there were thorns about this affectionate heart."

"Is there then a recipe?"

"Yes, and one so simple that I hesitate to give it to you. Instead of *struggling* against your poor friend, *struggle* against yourself; instead of *praying so much* that he may correct what does not depend upon his will to change, *pray* for *yourself* that you may become better; instead of *weeping*, smile, come what may; in a word, diminish the number of your own faults, and *become saintly*.

"A saint, a real saint is patient; and patience is like the woollen garments in which we clothe ourselves in winter, that we may not feel the cold. Have you ever dreamed of preventing the weather from being cold?

"A saint is *gentle;* and gentleness is the soft bulwark with which sanctity surrounds us to blunt the edge of sharp or unjust words which might rend our hearts.

"To labor for the amendment of others is often difficult and even impossible; to labor upon ourselves is always possible, and I add, *always efficacious.*"

"But is it not difficult *to be a saint?*"

"We have only to let the good God do with us simply as He wills, be a docile instrument in His hands."

VI.

AMEN! ALLELUIA!

These two words should be continually on the lips and in the heart of the Christian soul.

Amen, that is a submissive yes; *Alleluia*, that is a joyful thanksgiving.

Amen is the cry of the soul which wills all that God wills.

Alleluia is the cry of the soul which is happy in all that God permits.

Amen is the cry of the love which submits.

Alleluia is the cry of the love which goes to meet the will of God and loves it.

Amen is particularly the cry of the saints on earth.

Alleluia is the cry of the saints in heaven. And when a soul on earth, who has known how to say *Amen* learns to say also *Alleluia*, then there arises between God and this soul an ineffable union which leaves her in the deepest peace, and enables God to say to His angels what He said when He showed them His servant Job, "*See how she loves me!*"

**

Hear this hymn of one of God's suffering children obliged to be separated from her dying mother:

"To-day is Holy Saturday, *Alleluia!* My heart bleeds at the thought of my mother lying sick below while I am unable to be at her pillow; but God's will be done, *Alleluia!* I am suffering more than I did yesterday, but, *Alleluia!* This morning I raised blood several times, but God's will be ever praised, *Alleluia!* What awaits me? I know not. God knows, *Alleluia!*"

O then, my soul, love to repeat these cries which the lips are powerless to utter, and which can only come from a will which is wholly God's.

A storm of opposition, of calumny, of contempt, may be gathering about thee:
Amen! Alleluia!

Coldness, indifference, scorn may appear on every side:
Amen! Alleluia!

Thou art oppressed with a sense of abandonment, neglect, utter powerlessness, moral and physical.

Amen! Alleluia!

My God, when the saints shall offer Thee their labors, the martyrs their wounds, the virgins their hearts burning with love, what could I offer Thee? Come my crosses, come my trials little and great, for without ye I could not but blush before the saints and angels; my hands would be empty. Yes, come little crosses, you are all my wealth, my gold, my jewels! Come and help me to purchase heaven!

Amen! Alleluia!

***

We find in the *journal* of a *Christian woman* the following beautiful prayer, a moving commentary of the *Amen* and *Alleluia* of a loving soul:

" Will of my God, how bitter art thou to-day! The cross which I dreaded most is the one I carry; a cross without humiliation is incomplete; complete mine, my God, for nothing is wanting in it to humiliate me, to crucify me, to prostrate me; death alone could crush me more. Yet no, Lord, death to me would be better than life. But Thou willest that I should live to suffer; ah, to also love Thee! I love Thee then, my Lord, my God, in the midst of tears, but submissive tears.

"How numerous are my unanswered prayers! How long have I given and received nothing! The more I give myself to good works the more Thou seemest to afflict me, the more I confide in Thy providence the more it seems to abandon me! What then dost Thou wish of Thy poor creature, O my God? Thou who hast created her, willest Thou to annihilate her, to crush her like a fragile vase? No, Thou wouldst only clothe her in the garment of humiliation. Ah, Lord, Thou givest me then the mantle which Thou thyself didst wear. Clothed in this world like my God, I shall later share His robe of glory. Ah, yes, my God, for all, all things be ever praised and blessed!

"In twenty-four years, and even less, I shall no longer be here lowering my eyes before contemptuous glances and cutting words. I shall be with the angels and saints blessing the sorrowful moments of my life which shall have availed me the joys of Paradise. Oh, yes, for all, all things, my God, be praise and thanksgiving rendered Thee!"

Amen! Alleluia!

VII.

LITTLE DEVICES FOR RESTORING PEACE TO THE SOUL AND CAUSING IT TO ACQUIRE MERITS.

We are about to publish under this title a series of counsels which will complete those we have written under the title of *Little Offices*.

The *Little Devices* are more intimate, their direct end is to fill the soul with light, joy and peace; to make her accept with love the *portion* of *sadness* which God has left her, and to make her no longer regard as *thorns* but as *special blessings* the little miseries of life which at times grieve her so much:

Defects impossible to correct.

Exterior faults which are deeply humiliating.

Inability to do good which stifles every joyous impulse.

Failure which disheartens and discourages.

Oh, none of these, none of many other things, would we *take* from the soul, but we would make them a *subject of merit for heaven*, and even upon earth a *subject of continual thanksgiving to the good God.*

**

The end of these little devices is to teach us those means of gaining heaven invented by a few more industrious souls, which are not difficult to practise, only we do not think of them because no one has suggested them, and yet they are to the *soul's welfare* what the little *secrets of labor* invented by *skilful artisans* are to the *welfare of the body*.

It was in consoling a discouraged friend that we learned to appreciate all the *merciful kindness* in these *little miseries* which the good God has sown in all the hours of our life.

Permit us as introduction to relate this personal experience; it also may contain a useful lesson.

I found a poor friend in tears, and pressing his hand affectionately, I asked more by my manner than by words,

"Why are you troubled?"

"I cannot be *amiable*," he answered

with a simplicity which touched me, "and yet I feel the necessity of being so.

"I need to be amiable to *do good* to those about me, for without amiability my words are cold, my example fruitless, and I live in the midst of the loving members of my family without ever being able to reach one heart to place therein a fortifying thought. Yet God wishes that I should make those who love me happy.

"I need to be amiable to *be grateful*, for I feel their kindness without knowing how to thank them. I feel that they love me and are devoted to me, but I am unable to show them that I *appreciate* it! Oh, if you knew what a trial it is!

"I need to be amiable to *be virtuous* myself, for I live in a state of continual restraint which paralyzes my efforts, and leaves me unable to pray, to act, or to devote myself as I should!

"What I lack is not devotedness, nor

even *tact;* it is the *habitual smile,* the *manifest confidence, loving, gracious words.*"

I smiled at this naïve outpouring of a heart which I knew exaggerated its want of amiability, and drawing nearer to my good and pious friend, I said,

"Are you thus with the good God?"

"Oh, no," he answered quickly; "I am unrestrained with God, I am happy in His presence, for I feel that I love Him, and I can tell Him so. It is only with God that I *feel at ease;* with others, with every one I am afraid of being a burden! Oh, if you knew how hard it is!"

* *
*

I do not know what more I said to my friend, but when I left him he pressed my hand, and with a happy smile in the midst of his tears said, "*I thank you!*"

Then in the presence of God this simple prayer came involuntarily to my lips:

"I thank Thee, my God, for the salutary burden Thou hast sent this loving heart. Ah, if he felt that he was loved as he desires, *he would love creatures too much and forget Thee perhaps!* Leave him, yes, leave him his sorrow, but increase his strength, still hide from him the good his devotion does."

And I understood how the good God leaves about the most beautiful and the most delicate souls *exterior faults* that they may not be spoiled by vanity or sensuality; as the gardener places a thorny hedge about the tender plant to preserve it from all injury.

From these reflections came the labor we are about to begin.

We have spoken these things in the intimacy of friendship before writing them, and if we now publish them it is because we are sure there are other souls in the world who resemble those to whom God permitted us to do good.

* * *

Make our imperfections means of expiation and merit by bearing them as necessary crosses and refraining from even asking God to diminish them.

Each of us has imperfections and defects, sometimes *very apparent* ones.

It may be a bodily deformity, a want of regularity in the formation of our limbs, something ridiculous in our appearance or bearing, great difficulty in making ourselves understood and in comprehending others.

Sometimes it is a thoughtless disposition which in spite of our efforts makes us forgetful, a natural awkwardness which causes us to break or mar all that we touch.

Or it may be an irritable sensitiveness which causes us to see ill-will on every side, and makes us suspicious, a sharpness of manner which makes us appear unsociable. Oh, how good all these are as means of expiation and merit!

Certainly there is *nothing culpable* in this awkwardness, in these continual blunders, in those comical faults into which we involuntarily fall, and which excite the laughter of others; nor even in natural brusqueness, and the sharp words which, escaping us in spite of ourselves, deeply humiliate us, and which we would correct at any price. But are we convinced that God had a merciful design in leaving us under the weight of these continual humiliations?

Poor soul, perhaps without this *exterior rudeness* which estranges persons from you, and obliges you to live more retired, you would have given yourself up to the affections of your *too loving heart* and you would have been lost.

Perhaps but for this timidity which prevents you from coming forward and manifesting your ideas, you would have wished to be first everywhere, to rule everywhere, and perhaps with the flattery and adulation you received you would have been lost.

Perhaps but for these continual blunders which excite a smile, and therefore cause you to keep apart from others, you would have wished to speak, to counsel, to direct, and with imprudent counsel causing *many falls* you would have been lost.

Then let us endure ourselves as we *are*, as God made us. There is in this habitual state *a continual cross* which is like a thorny hedge on the border of our path, keeping us within it and leading us surely to our end.

O happy constraint! happy obstacles!

Some strong souls in their generosity go so far as to ask God to *increase their imperfections;* we, doubtless, shall not go as far as this; let us correct ourselves if we can; but if, in spite of our efforts, we cannot be rid of this *burden* which God has placed upon our mind, our disposition, or our heart, oh, let us heartily accept it, and sometimes even bless God for it!

VIII.

SIMPLE COUNSELS TO A YOUNG GIRL.

Yes, very simple. Heed them, dear child, and may they gradually penetrate your soul like dew into the calyx of the flower.

They are merely stated, but why may not you in your little room, all by yourself, endeavor to develop them in writing? The labor of another is never as effective for us as the work we do ourselves.

These are the counsels:

Distrust a too sudden friendship.

Distrust a pleasure which moves you too deeply.

Distrust a word which troubles you or suddenly charms you.

Distrust a book which sets you dreaming.

Distrust a thought which you would not confide to your mother.

Place these counsels at the foot of your crucifix; and sometimes as you read each line ask yourself, *Why?*

Guardian angels of children, to whom we address ourselves, whisper to their souls, tell them the reason for *this distrust* which may appear to them exaggerated.

IX.

RECIPES FOR NEVER WEARYING FRIENDS.

This recipe was composed by a person whose life was for a long time tormented, spoiled, poisoned by the minute care and attention lavished upon her by the too ardent affection of a sincerely devoted but indiscreet relative.

There is a medium in all things, even in the manifestation of affection, even in the bestowal of *kind attentions*, even in the removal of *little miseries*.

This recipe has but four very clear and very precise articles. Here they are:

1. *I will always leave my friend still something to desire.* If he begs me to come to see him three times, I will go twice. He will dream at night of my third visit, and will receive me the more cordially on the morrow. It is so pleasant to feel one's self wanted, and very hard to fear one's self importunate!

2. *I will serve my friend as far as he wishes, but no more.* An officious friendship is always inconvenient, and a prodigality of even the most beautiful sentiments renders those insupportable. Devotion does not consist in doing for one's friend *all that can be done*, but simply in doing *all that may be agreeable or useful to him*, and further we must let him discover for himself, rather than show him what we do. As we all pas-

sionately love our liberty we hold to our little *eccentricities;* we do not like to have that arranged with too much order which we naturally leave a little out of *order;* we would not even have too much *care* taken of us.

I will *busy myself with my own affairs, and a little with those of my friend, but very little.* This rule will infallibly result usefully. First of all, by busying myself with my own affairs I will *complete* them, and afford my friend an opportunity to do the same with his, and each will be satisfied. If he call me to his assistance I will go through fire to help him; but if he does not call me I will feel that I am obliging him infinitely and myself as well by not interfering in any way. If, however, I can help him *without his knowledge,* when I perceive that he would not ask me, I shall always do it.

I will allow my friend the liberty to think and act as he pleases in things indifferent. Why should I force him to think and act with me? Am I a type of the good and beautiful? And is it not absurd to imagine that another thinks and acts ill, the moment he differs from me? Doubtless I shall not always assure him that *he is right,* but I shall generally permit him to believe it.

**

Try this recipe, and I assure you you will keep your friends a long time.

X.

BEFORE GOD, BEFORE GOD ALONE.

Do not these words create about your soul a calm and kindly atmosphere?

Before God! The words suggest a protecting refuge, a strengthening dew, a luminous, inebriating ray!

Oh, then, why this continual search

for some one to *see* me, to *comprehend* me, to *appreciate* me, to *applaud* me?

That human eye which I seek is the burning ray which pales the most delicate colors of a precious fabric. It is the damp wind which softens, bends and withers the yet frail stem.

Every action done to *be seen* has lost its freshness in the eyes of God. It is a flower already withered by having passed through several hands, and has become scarcely presentable.

O my poor soul! be the flower of the desert which grows and thrives and blossoms because God wills it, untroubled whether the passing bird sees it, or the whistling wind scatters its scarcely formed leaves.

You must not, doubtless, abandon family intercourse nor that of friendship or society; but know how to reserve each day a few moments for *yourself alone*, and for *God alone*.

Know particularly how to perform some actions with the thought that they shall never be known to *any one but God*.

Oh, how good it is to desire God alone as witness!

It is *sanctity* in its highest degree.

It is happiness in its most exquisite sense.

It is the best founded *assurance* of one day entering heaven.

The mother reserving for her child what is most precious and delicate, the child working *in secret* to surprise its mother, knows no joy purer or greater than does the worker in her little room daily living *before God*, whom alone she desires to please; or than the charitable heart sending to a poor family an alms bearing only the simple words, *From God*.

***

We found in some fragments of old papers the following notes written by an unknown hand:

I have just been told of a poor, sick woman. I gave *twenty cents* for her, I owed it as an example, but now, my God, for Thee, Thee alone, I am going to send her secretly a dollar which I shall take from my monthly allowance.

To-morrow Henry is to come to see me, poor Henry whom I loved so much, and who has grown so indifferent to his old friend; he sought to injure me, and he does not know that I am aware of it. Grant me to remember, O my God, that I have pardoned him all, and help me to receive him kindly. Thou alone canst know what I have suffered.

What a good day yesterday was, good for heaven, for, alas! my poor heart suffered much. Yesterday was a feast day. The snow kept every one by their fireside, and I was alone!

Oh, yes, my poor heart suffered much yesterday! but my soul was happy. I began to talk with God as if I saw Him, and gradually my heart was cheered, and I spent the evening *alone with the good God*. I know not what I said, what I wrote, but the memory of yesterday has remained with me like a stimulating perfume.

Perhaps at the last day of a life full of activity, energy, and labor there will remain to be rewarded but those little actions done only *before God.* My God, teach me to *live* before Thee, to *labor* before Thee, to suffer before Thee, to act sometimes before Thee *alone!*

XI.

Oh, how the saints know how to love! "Friends ought to manage to die at the same time," says Fénélon. "In every other respect my soul is weak and poor," writes St. Francis of Sales, "but my affection is very tenacious. There is no one in the world whose heart is more tender for his friends, nor who feels more keenly the pain of being separated from them."

My God, give me a saint for a friend!

XII.

LITTLE DEVICES FOR RESTORING PEACE TO THE SOUL AND CAUSING IT TO ACQUIRE MERIT.

II.

Enrich ourselves spiritually with the good and the labor of others.

This device is for you, dear souls, who have received as portion from God but little exterior *savoir faire*, little *knowledge of business*, and who are employed in material labors doubtless very necessary, but regarded by the world with disdain; for you, who sometimes sigh before God for your *little ability* to labor for the salvation of souls, for your *nothingness*, your *timidity*, your complete want of success; poor *lay sisters* of communities who think they do nothing for souls; *poor sick ones*, only fit to give trouble, you say; poor unfortunates deformed by nature, who fear to appear anywhere, or offer yourselves for any service; poor aged ones worn out in labor who can only creep on to the end, and who believe yourselves an encumbrance in a household.

Let us admit as true all these thoughts which grieve and overwhelm you. Do you not still possess a *heart with which to love?* Then it is with this heart, ever young because of its goodness, that you can *be useful to others* and *enrich yourself* more than formerly perhaps.

***

1. Love those who labor more than you and better than you. *Rejoice* in their success.

Offer God each day their labors and their fatigue, and the glory which springs from their works.

Do you think that at Nazareth there were not long hours during which Mary said to God, " May the actions of Jesus be mine; may the sufferings of Jesus be mine; may the thoughts of Jesus be mine"? And during these hours of union, do you think Mary did not merit?

At Mass, have you not seen the priest raising the sacred host and the chalice, and offering it to God, adoring, loving, glorifying *through Jesus* and *with Jesus?* That is what you must do; say, *My God, I offer Thee the labor of this priest who devotes himself* to the conversion of souls, of this religious who is spending her strength in teaching, of that missionary in a far country whom I do not know, but who is dying for Thee neglected in a strange land.

2. Contribute according to your employment to the *material welfare* of those who labor directly for souls, with the thought that by making them stronger and happier their labors may be multiplied to the greater glory of God.

You who are charged with the *cleanliness* of the house, let everything shine with neatness! Toiling minds will find in the midst of this order a charm and comfort which shall redouble their force and give new life to their zeal.

You who are charged with the *preparation of the food*, do all you can to make it wholesome and strengthening; upon this depends health; upon health exterior labor; upon this exterior labor depends in part the salvation of souls; and before God you shall have a large share in the good which may be done.

*_**

You who can only *pray* and *suffer*, pray and suffer for others. Have you ever witnessed those scenes on the seashore when divers go to the bottom of the sea in search of riches sunken there? While the divers are laboring below there are men on shore who continually send them the necessary air by means of ingenious mechanism. So it is with us who labor for souls. Grace is the necessary means of success, and this grace is only obtained by prayer. While we preach, while we teach, and while we are absorbed in material labor pray, pray for us! Perhaps the largest share of the success of our mission with souls shall be due to you who believe yourselves useless.

XIII.

SIMPLE COUNSELS TO YOUNG GIRLS.

Confide in Your Mother.

A young girl is naturally open.
She is a flower diffusing perfume.
A bird sending forth its song.
A star shedding light upon the hearth.

And when the flower closes, when the bird is silent, when the star no longer shines, a *shadow* falls.

O children, when you fold up your

heart, when you close your lips, and your eyes fall before your mother's glance, you know whence the shadow comes. The angels in passing leave no clouds.

This shadow is a *flattering word* willingly listened to and repeated softly to yourself; it is a sentiment of envy excited in your soul by a more striking toilet, or by a more brilliant success; it is a page read in spite of the cries of conscience; it is perhaps a few lines received without your mother's knowledge which have caused you a culpable emotion.

Poor child, poor child, see whether your conscience does not whisper to you these lines, which sprang from a first remorse:

Words that my ears ne'er knew until to-day
Have left me no more a maiden free from guile;
The blush that came when first I heard their sound,
Was quickly changed, alas! into a smile.

Ah, if you wish to become again *a maiden free from guile*, if you wish not to be lost irrevocably,

CONFIDE IN YOUR MOTHER.

There are secrets which your mother alone should know, *secrets of the heart.*

How closely the hearts of mother and child resemble each other when they are both pious, and how readily above all they understand each other!

You will not need to say much; the tone of your voice in the one word, *Mother*, will tell her there is something to see, something to ask, something to heal, something to strengthen, and be sure she has at her command treasures of love, of an all-powerful love.

If you knew the harm you do yourself by concealing your heart from your mother!

⁎

CONFIDE IN YOUR CONFESSOR.

There are secrets which your confessor alone should know, the *secrets of your soul*.

There is a divine radiance about the confessor in the tribunal of penance. Approach him as respectfully as you would the Holy Table. God is there also, though in a different manner, and when kneeling before him you feel a hesitation which is certainly pardonable. Let the word *Father* with which you address him reanimate your heart to confidence. Simply expose your soul to him; tell him your weaknesses, your fears, your allurements, your falls; tell him particularly of your desires to do better, and then listen to his counsels.

Let there be no hesitation in your obedience. What he forbids, avoid; what he counsels, practise.

Frequently he may tell you, " *Go to*

your mother." Then go to your mother; go to her with more confidence than ever.

The guardian angel of the priest and the guardian angel of a mother always understand each other. Christian mothers know this; and many times when troubled at sight of clouds on her child's brow a mother even before asking any question will say, "*Go to confession, my child, and return to your mother!*"

CONFIDE IN JESUS IN THE EUCHARIST.

Confidence here does not consist in words; it is *union*.

And how sweet, how intimate, how touching is this confidence in Jesus in the Eucharist! Without speech we are understood; we make no effort to be seen; we feel that we are known.

Oh, draw near to the Holy Table, my child; approach it frequently. Holy Communion is the continuance and the support of that *joy* which confidence in your mother gave you, and of the *peace* which came to you with the words of the priest.

Yes, receive Holy Communion; and when your confessor has given you permission do not stay away from the Holy Table except for grave, very grave reasons. Do you not feel that there are *aspirations* in your heart which Jesus alone can satisfy? Do you not feel that there are *voids* which He alone can fill? Do you not feel that there are *weaknesses* which He alone can strengthen?

And you, poor children, who have no mother! Oh, I understand the pang which rends your heart as you read these lines which tell of that *heart to heart* converse of mother and child.

Let me only repeat to you to-day the words of Jesus on the Cross, giving us all the Blessed Virgin, *Behold thy mother.*

XIV.

SANCTIFICATION.

Sanctification for the majority of souls is an *edifice* formed of grains of sand and drops of water under the direction of the *great architect* who is God.

These grains of sand and drops of water God gathers about us and softly whispers to our heart, *To work, my child; build; the labor is easy; I will help thee."*

And this labor which He asks is simple *fidelity*, not to lose one grain of sand or drop of water, and to transform them by an act of the will into those materials which are called *virtues.*

∗∗∗

Would you know what are these *grains of sand and drops of water?*

They are those little *nothings* with

which life is sown and which are called *inevitable contradictions, depression for which we can assign no cause, a duty loved yesterday, and to-day a burden, the sudden joy of an affectionate word or an unlooked-for pleasure, an obstacle which paralyzes our efforts, the surprise of a humiliation, an abandonment which grieves the heart.*

All little *nothings*, it is true; but *nothings* which form the tissue of every life which is *sweet and tranquil and free from grave misfortunes.*

Behold the *materials* of your sanctification; restless soul, eager to know what God asks of you, behold what God furnishes you.

Would you know what you must furnish on your part?

A little more peace in labor, a little more delicacy of conscience, a little more kindliness of manner, and sweetness of words, a lit-

tle stronger effort to control your disquiet, a little more patience to wait, a little more good-nature in receiving others, a little more goodness in excusing others.

⁂

Behold on the one side God and the materials He offers you—on the other side yourself and the tools possessed by your will.

Set yourself to work, and to fill the moments of each day you will obtain:

A dangerous glance repressed, a malicious smile arrested, a line interrupted in prompt obedience, a sensual memory stifled, a cherished letter rapidly read and a second reading sacrificed, an ill-natured feeling courageously conquered, an unsympathetic person received with simple kindness, importunity or ennui borne with sweetness, an impulse of temper or a movement of passion promptly put down, a useless expense curtailed, a cloud of sadness gently dissipated, a too natural joy tempered, fear calmed by a glance at the Divine Guest and Protector in our heart, a fiat slowly and lovingly repeated in the midst of the most violent attack of sadness or moral suffering, a painful duty continued courageously to the end.

Each of these acts is a stone added every moment perhaps to the edifice of your sanctification.

And each one is called an *act of virtue*, the *money* which buys heaven.

***

But is there not an unattractive, continual and difficult constraint in this?

Studied *in detail* these multiplied acts are alarming; *in practice* they cost little, and are accomplished in the midst of peace and joy.

To this end we need but *seriously oblige ourselves to do to those about us all the good we can, to say to them all the kind words we can, to look upon God as a father whom we truly love and whom we would never displease, finally to regard our soul and our heart as a child whom we would render beautiful, good and worthy.*

I insist upon this last thought, too little known. Why not regard our soul and heart as *a child* whom God has confided to us with the mission to render it very pure and very good?

Does the care bestowed upon our body ever weary us? And my poor heart, how I neglect thee, and how little I am troubled for thy health or thy real welfare.

XV.

LITTLE DEVICES TO RESTORE PEACE TO THE SOUL AND TO CAUSE IT TO ACQUIRE MERITS.

III.

Make of our Necessary Trials a Penance of Love by Accepting Them with Resignation.

Who has not daily trials to endure? Who does not daily feel the sting of suffering, sometimes in his members, sometimes in his heart, sometimes in his imagination, sometimes in his mind, *uneasiness, ennui, vague fears, humiliation, contradiction, separation from a loved one, ingratitude, irritation, the loss of an object endeared by sweet memories?*

All this is *permitted* by God; I say more, *sent* by God to *purify* us, to *detach* us, to lead us to have *recourse to Him*, in a word to *sanctify us*.

Oh, if we thought of this how we should daily at our awaking prepare our soul to receive each of its trials, and how from time to time we should say in the words of a Christian soul, "*O my dear little trials, how I love you!*"

*_**

There is no penance more efficacious to satisfy God, nor more appropriate to our nature and our wants, than the trials sent us by God, whether they come directly from Him or whether they come through creatures.

God as a *skilful physician* knows the evil within us, the evil which daily gains ground in our heart and would end by corrupting it, and He *chooses* the remedy appropriate to the evil.

As a loving father He chooses the gentlest remedy for His beloved child, and He proportions the dose to its strength, and He waits the best moment to administer it.

As a just judge, He never imposes more than the penance merited, and this He also lightens when it is accepted with love!

O my God, why have I not sooner reflected on all these truths! If during the fifteen, twenty, thirty years that I have lived under Thy gentle Providence I had permitted Thee to do Thy will how beautiful and devoted *my soul* would be! how docile and kind my *disposition!* how ardent my *charity!*

Perhaps, my God, I should be already in heaven for I should have attained the degree of virtue, of love, of purity, which Thou awaitest to place me near, very near Thee!

O my God, what I have not done, help me to do!

Render me docile to the hand which has the mission to correct me.

Render me *strong* in humiliation, neglect, disapproval, and do not permit me to be discouraged or to murmur.

Make me *kind* to those who do not love me, who think ill of me, who speak ill of me, and give me an opportunity to do them good.

**

Penances chosen by ourselves are doubtless *good*, but they have in them something which flatters *self-love*. The demon whispers to us, *You* did that, and sometimes a smile of self-satisfaction destroys much of the merit o these voluntary penances. Then, with the exception of the *penance imposed by a confessor*, are we sure that God wishes *those we perform in the time we perform them, in the manner we perform them?*

But the penances sent by God, these we are sure are *needful* to us, that they are needed *as long as they last!* and that they *effect in our body, our heart, our soul all the good God wills they should do!*

O my God! when then shall I know how to thank Thee for *all things?* When then can I say before humiliation, physical and moral suffering, separation, enduring weariness, what a Christian mother said before the lifeless body of a beloved daughter, *Behold the best day of my life, I cannot suffer more!*

XVI.

"I feel kind to-day, my God. Oh, grant that *something may be asked of me,* for to-morrow I may be ill-humored and then I may no longer desire to be generous, or I may give ungraciously. Thou knowest, my God, that I must needs *give* to resemble Thee, and to please Thee!"

This prayer of a Christian soul I also address to Thee my God!

Oh, render me *very happy* sometimes, that I may be *very kind*, and then direct one of Thy hungry poor to me and tell him to show me his need.

Send me a sorrowful heart, and let it expose its grief to me.

Send me a troubled embittered mind, and tell it to confide its troubles to me.

And when I shall have given *an alms*, *a word of peace*, *a word of love*, smile upon me as the master smiles upon his faithful servant, and let me resume my somewhat suffering, laborious life.

XVII.

THE SOUL'S THIRST.

What wouldst thou, poor parched soul? What wouldst thou to-day?

Ah! I know the cry which comes from the depth of thy nature every hour in every situation: *To love! to love!*

Why these sighs, these aspirations, these desires? *Act*, my poor soul! Love is not sighs nor desires which can no more satisfy thee than *smoke* may satisfy the hungry beggar.

Love is the *gift of self*. To love is to place at the disposition of others, for their alleviation, their instruction, their happiness and their sanctification, *all that God has lent us*.

To love is to do each moment, each day and for each person with whom Providence gives us any intercourse, what Jesus would do were He in our place surrounded by the same persons, and having the same means we have.

Oh, how He would have loved you all, even though, with a feeling of ill will, you had withdrawn from Him and avoided His presence.

How tender He would have been in word, how kind in manner, how patient in the pain you caused Him, how humble and modest in the good He lavished upon you.

How readily He would have pardoned, begun again on the morrow what he failed to accomplish the previous day, how He would have sought to appease you, to draw near to you to do you good.

How He would have prayed for you every day, suffered something for you every day to win you to God.

How He would have hidden your faults, excused your failings, repaired your neglects; how kindly He would have spoken of you, and how He would have sought to make you loved and appreciated by all.

This is *love;* it is not satisfied with desires, with dreams, *it gives itself completely*

It makes no choice, it *gives itself to all.*

It does not calculate, it *never ceases to give.*

*

Let us not imagine that Jesus continually worked miracles to gain hearts, to render service, to give pleasure and lead souls to God.

It was not the angels who performed for Mary and Joseph those duties of a submissive industrious child which entailed material fatigue, no, it was Jesus who really wearied Himself in the labor.

The union of the divine with the human nature did not prevent the heart of Jesus from being wounded by a want of consideration, from being hurt by a harsh word, from being grieved by ingratitude, and yet neither the treason of Judas, nor the brusqueness of the apostles, nor the ingratitude of the Jews ever for a moment cooled His love.

*

Jesus, Jesus, I would love like Thee!

Behold thyself, my soul, with thy ardor, thy enthusiasm, thy desire to suddenly attain the end.

But know that thou canst really *love*, that is, *devote thyself to all in all things always*, only in as far as thou art *pure and docile* in God's hands, and this means the continual accomplishment of duty and the smiling acceptance of the trials which accompany it.

Then it will doubtless be thou who shalt act and who shalt have the merit of thy actions, but it will be God who *impels* thee, who *sustains* thee, who *uses* thee, who in a measure unable to *love His creatures in a material manner*, chooses thee to replace Him, and thou, a frail little creature, wilt be the *good God made visible*.

⁎
⁎

Oh, what a good and strengthening thought!

It was naïvely expressed by a poor woman, whom a member of the St. Vincent of Paul Society was taking care of. Unable to express the feelings of her heart she exclaimed one day in a transport of gratitude, Oh, sir, *if there were two good Gods you would be one.*

I wish to be a *good God*, for God is love, and I wish to love, O my God!

XVIII.

HOW SOULS ARE CURED.

I know few words harder to the heart of a priest than the words, *I cannot!* coldly uttered by a soul of whom God asks a sacrifice.

It may be a sacrifice of the *will* necessary to accept a position or a manner of living which thwarts one's taste, destroys the projects of self-love: *I cannot!* the soul answers.

It may be a sacrifice of the *heart*, the renouncement of an affection already culpable or about to become so, and which charms and allures: *I cannot!* the soul answers. Oh, with a soul which resists like this and intrenches itself, so to speak, behind double bolts with the cold and icy words: *I cannot,* what is to be done?

Yet its salvation is at stake, and it does not see, poor blind one! where it is being led by *this disobedience* to a superior who has a right to command, or by this *sensual affection* which gradually destroys the candor and reserve which make it so beautiful in the eyes of the angels.

*

One day a young girl kneeling in the confessional before a priest continued insensible to the earnest words of her spiritual father, who prayed her to sacrifice a guilty affection. There was the beginning of a struggle in her conscience, but she stifled it with the words, *I cannot!*

"My child," said the priest, "be frank; is it *I cannot or I will not?*"

Silence.

"Tell me, my child, have you the courage to say to me, and to say to the good God, *I will not?*"

Grace began to do its work; the young girl, more moved than she would appear, could hardly restrain her tears.

"Oh, I would, I would, I wish to, Father, but *I cannot!*"

"My child, will you do what I am going to ask you in the name of Jesus Christ, or rather what Jesus Christ asks you through me?"

"Father—"

"Say simply, *yes* or *no*.

"Yes, Father!"

"Then go before the Blessed Sacrament, and holding your beads in your hand, repeat these words, slowly enunciating each syllable:"

"*The good God, my Master and my Father, wishes me to renounce this affection,* which leads to my ruin, and I say that I cannot, but in reality I will not.

"These words, which you feel are *true*, repeat slowly *twenty* times at least on your beads, pausing each time a few seconds to let them gently sink into your soul.

***

"Then with the same slowness repeat twenty times more the following words:

"*My God who canst do all things, have pity on me! Do not punish me, but give me the will, the strength and the means to renounce this affection which displeases Thee.*

"As between the first words, pause a few seconds each time after you have uttered them. Then twenty times more and still more slowly say:

"*My God, who hast been so long calling me, awaiting me, urging me, and whom I ever resist! my God, pardon me the pain I give Thy fatherly heart and make me docile!*

"At the end of this third invocation

ask the intercession of Mary with the prayer:

"'O my sovereign! O my mother!' and making the sign of the cross as if receiving God's blessing quietly retire.

"During all the week let this be your morning and evening meditation.

"Go now, my child. God bless you!"

Before the end of the week the poor child returned; returned with a sore but generous heart. "Father," she said, unconscious that she was repeating the words of the Apostle conquered by grace, "*Father, what will you that I do?*"

She was told her duty, and she did it.

O priests of Jesus Christ! let us remember the sweet, gentle, but strong and penetrating power of submissive, humble prayer.

Let us remember that about the Holy

Eucharist is a divine atmosphere formed of graces infinitely powerful to first *soften*, then *penetrate*, and finally *transform* souls.

Send there your sick, almost hopeless souls as physicians send to certain salutary waters those to whom their remedies are useless.

Yes, dear souls, who cannot overcome your habits, who have not the strength to be resigned, to submit, to accept what is sent, go to *Jesus* in the *Eucharist;* gently pour out your heart to Him in a short prayer, slowly repeated, and let the merciful power of Jesus drop by drop penetrate your soul. The continual dropping of water upon a stone always tells upon it in the end and softens it.

XIX.

A FEW THOUGHTS UPON THE CONFESSION OF PIOUS PERSONS.

Confide in your confessor, Golden Sands tells us, and the sweet words which developed this counsel made ample provision for the *needs of the heart*. Ah, there are times when this provision must needs be ample—very ample! It is a means of sanctification but *is it sanctity itself?*

This very wise question suggested the following thoughts.

They may appear *somewhat severe* on a first reading, but we pray you souls who sincerely desire to amend to read them again quietly and let their light penetrate you, and you will find them simply *true*.

⁎
⁎

Many think they have acquitted themselves of everything when they have resolved to *confess their sins*, and with the majority penance

Eucharist is a divine atmosphere formed of graces infinitely powerful to first *soften*, then *penetrate*, and finally *transform* souls.

Send there your sick, almost hopeless souls as physicians send to certain salutary waters those to whom their remedies are useless.

Yes, dear souls, who cannot overcome your habits, who have not the strength to be resigned, to submit, to accept what is sent, go to *Jesus* in the *Eucharist;* gently pour out your heart to Him in a short prayer, slowly repeated, and let the merciful power of Jesus drop by drop penetrate your soul. The continual dropping of water upon a stone always tells upon it in the end and softens it.

XIX.

A FEW THOUGHTS UPON THE CONFESSION OF PIOUS PERSONS.

Confide in your confessor, Golden Sands tells us, and the sweet words which developed this counsel made ample provision for the *needs of the heart.* Ah, there are times when this provision must needs be ample—very ample! It is a means of sanctification but *is it sanctity itself?*

This very wise question suggested the following thoughts.

They may appear *somewhat severe* on a first reading, but we pray you souls who sincerely desire to amend to read them again quietly and let their light penetrate you, and you will find them simply *true.*

**

Many think they have acquitted themselves of everything when they have resolved to *confess their sins,* and with the majority penance and amendment consists simply in making an *exact confession.*

**

After a retreat people say, *I have been to confession*, and imagine *everything is done; I confessed everything, now I am satisfied,* they add, and that which has occupied them most has been the effort to remember their sins, and perhaps to find terms to express them.

No, the *avowal of one's sins* is not conversion, it is only a means. Conversion is *turning another way,* it is withdrawing one's heart from the midst of amusements, frivolities, creatures to which we have yielded it, to bring it to God, and to leave it under His dependence.

**

The important part of confession then is not merely to confess your sins, but to *abandon* them; and when we are sincerely resolved to correct ourselves of a fault we always find courage to confess it. The courage to confess a fault does not always give the resolution to commit it no more.

**

There would be fewer scrupulous souls if people confessed their sins only after avoiding the occasion of them.

**

People talk too much in confession. If they would simply state their sin as it is, as it appears to them; if their desire was not only to be rid of it, but to expiate it by confessing it, how few words they would need to tell it!

***

The useless details, the list of imperfections with which people usually begin their confession, are a prelude to gently prepare the confessor and half divert his attention from what they are going to tell him later. Doubtless they do not do this deliberately, but they act thus *instinctively*.

***

There is no action it would seem which ought to confound vanity more than confession, and there is none perhaps in which there are more refinements of vanity. Who acknowledges *that he himself sought the sin*, and does he not, on the contrary, allow it to be understood that the *sin came to him?*

***

God is not always the One of whom we think first in our resolution to go to confession. The fittingness of a great feast, the desire to be rid of a heavy burden, are more frequent motives with us than the desire to amend.

Are there not souls who take the resolution to go to confession just as certain persons resolve to pay their debts? They pay not with the idea of contracting no more debt. Alas! it is sometimes quite the contrary ... they get rid of one debt which begins to be irksome that they may have the credit to contract another.

If I were asked which of the two, the confessor or the penitent, was most enlightened on the *nature* of the sin confessed, and particularly on the satisfaction required, I should not always say it was the confessor. The person, for example, who, after confessing that she reads frivolous books, or that she takes pleasure in somewhat dangerous conversation, adds that she does *not see any harm therein*, certainly does not think so, but she would like to have her confessor tell her so.

A woman who is now truly pious thus relates one of her confessions from which she dated her conversion:

My confessions were an apology for my best actions in which were intermingled a few very innocent peccadilloes, and my good confessor who did not divine me wept with admiration of my virtues. I would not have left him for all the world, even were he the cause of my damnation. We only leave confessors who humble us. But the good God had pity on me; He took him from me, and after many tears shed in public I chose a priest who had a great reputation for sanctity and talent.   That was what I needed.

The first time I made my confession to him he heard me without interruption, he let me quietly proceed with my eulogy interspersed with the most interesting imperfections, and when I had finished he told me to return in a *month*.

A month, Father! but I go to confession every week!

That is very often.

Oh, Father, it is not too often for a sinner like me.

I am not aware that you are a sinner; I have only seen perfections in you.

Yet I have confessed to you impatience, distractions, quick temper.

Yes, yes, things that you would be very sorry not to have; but see, how do you fulfil the duties of your state?

My state! but, Father—

But, madam, have you read the *Introduction to the Devout Life by St. Francis of Sales?*

No.

Read it and then return.

I left the confessional furious, saying to myself, That man has never confessed a lady of society, or he understands nothing of the spiritual life.

How was it that I went back to him? God led me. I was a long time understanding *humility*, and my good Father's strong words, Do not say *I am a sinner*, but act with the serious conviction that you *really* are a *sinner*.

His great, his only maxim was, *Every confession should increase fidelity to God, docility of character, leading us to greater consideration for the wishes of others, particularly when they thwart our own.*

XX.

HAVE YOU YOUR PHOTOGRAPH?

Singular question at the head of a chapter supposed to contain counsels for the *happiness and sanctification of life!*

To advise one to have one's photograph taken, is it not counselling *a little vanity?* And even if vanity counts for something in the *happiness of life* how can you say it enters into what forms the matter of its *sanctification?*

And yet this, yes, this is our counsel

of to-day, and given with reflection: *Have your photograph.*

Because *our photograph,* a faithful reproduction of our countenance, is also a more faithful reproduction perhaps of our soul; and if it be well done it may give us excellent counsels.

I.

Let us state first this axiom which no one will doubt.

Every one sitting for his photograph assumes the position which he thinks suits him best or simply is most flattering; the pose which makes him appear not as he really is, but such as he believes he is or would like to be.

This reflection was made some time ago, and the spiritual observer who uttered it proves it thus:

If you do not wish to study yourself, study through their photographs *such and such* persons whom you know intimately, better than you know yourself —the bad side of course.

Do you not say to yourself as you behold that fine smile, What a bright face she seems to have, if I didn't know her, I would really say. . . .

And this one; see her with her eyes raised to heaven! She has the air of an inspired prophetess. Yet . . .

Alas! And you? . . . Ah, if we wanted to be malicious!

II.

Place before you your photograph, taken at that happy age from eight to ten, when one appears free from affectation, good, naïve and confiding; a sweet, radiant little face, frank, half open mouth, clear bright eyes in which there is no fear, and through which you can read the very depths of the soul.

Is it not a pleasing picture?

Place beside it your photograph taken from *sixteen* to *twenty*. There is no longer the same candor, the same simplicity; there is a certain grace doubtless which would attract the eyes of strangers, but you yourself—do you not see behind that rather forced smile *a desire to excite admiration*, and perhaps an *effort to pose?*

Does it not make you a little ashamed?

Beside the first two place your photograph taken at that age when the breath of disenchantment, thank God! has passed over the illusions of youth, or experience and sorrow, alas! have ripened your life.

The face has lost the delicacy of its features, the lips have a rigid sad expression, the eyes do not look out so eagerly, as if they feared to *see too much* or *shrank from being seen*, and you ask yourself, *Is it really I?*

Does it not sadden you a little?

III.

Recollect yourself a moment before these pictures, contemplate them calmly, and little by little a multitude of the *purest, most touching, most salutary memories* will press into your mind.

Let them penetrate your heart, and if there be still any life there—life from above—your heart will be moved, deeply moved, and perhaps you will exclaim:

O my first youth !

O my naïve confidence !

O my first communion !

O my mother !

Ah! perhaps bitter regrets will arise in your heart.

Ah ! if I could begin over again !

IV.

And now be silent for a moment and listen Perhaps an ironical voice from out the picture cruelly whispers, *You have aged, you have aged*, but there come from it good counsels also:

"Oh! how everything has passed away, murmur the lips that were so fresh at *twelve*. Who would recognize to-day the careless, happy, innocent young girl of other times? Show this portrait to your most intimate friends. *Who among them would know it?*

Yes, it has fled ! The freshness of *twelve* will never come back to these features, but if you wish *it may bloom again in your soul !*

Your youth has faded, vanished forever, whispers the serious, grave face of this portrait. Cast from you then those illusions of self-love which tell you you are unchanged, and which impel you to speak and act and dress with a youthfulness unbecoming your years!

Live as becomes your age, spend your life carefully for but a small portion remains to you, and seek to make it useful.

You can no longer be *sought* as you were at twenty, you can always be *esteemed* and remain *worthy*.

Remember, remember that you are speeding onward, onward to God.

XXI.

The gate of heaven is very narrow, very low. Therefore see those who quietly glide through it:

The *humble* because they are lowly.

The *poor* because they have nothing.

The *obedient* because they know how to bend.

The *pure of heart* because they hold to nothing.

The *charitable*, unburdened with the possessions of which they have despoiled themselves to give to others.

The *patient*, for their little daily sufferings have lessened their stature.

XXII.

MEMORIAL FOR THE CHILDREN OF MARY.

Here, dear children of Mary, is the little memorial for which you asked.

Place it each morning before your eyes at the beginning of your day, just as we place a lighted lamp on the border of a path we are going to pursue, that it may light our steps.

It will be a *guide* ever keeping *God, God alone* before you as the end to which you must tend, leading you on to *Him* from hour to hour, and bringing you back to *Him* if you wander for a moment.

It will be the voice of your good angel in the evening which shall say to you: *Thou hast been faithful, go to thy rest in peace, God is pleased with thee;* or perhaps the voice may say: *Thou didst forget thyself, ask pardon, then go to thy rest in peace, to-morrow thou wilt do better!*

WHAT I MUST DO.

I.

FOR GOD.

Prayers.
- Uttered slowly with recollection and constancy.
- Peaceful, calm, resigned;
- Simple, humble, confiding;
- *Ever* respectful and as loving *as we can offer.*
- Charitable—have I not always about me opportunities of giving them to others, of bestowing them in thanksgiving?

Be submissive.
- To my position and to my duties:
  - They come from God, He imposes them upon me;
  - They bind me to God, to neglect them is to estrange myself from God.
- To the guide of my soul:
  - He has received from God light for my guidance, goodness from God to help me.
- To my parents:
  - Their authority is from God.
- To events:
  - They are prepared and sent by God.

Labor.
- Joyously undertaken,
- Perseveringly continued,
- Peacefully interrupted and resumed.

Rest and bodily care.
- In the presence of God,
- Under the protection of God.

II.

FOR MY NEIGHBOR.

Good example.
- By my modest bearing, and my simple but neat and suitable dress;
- By my habitual cheerfulness and repose;
- By condescending to all that can give him pleasure;
- By my fidelity in accomplishing all that is prescribed me.

Good words.
- Of unaffected zeal,
- Of encouragement,
- Of consolation,
- Of peace,
- Of joy,
- Of friendship.

Good actions.

Services rendered:
- By my alms,
- By my industry,
- By my influence.

Evil repaired:
- By excusing, justifying, protecting, defending;
- By concealing faults and omissions, and, if possible, repairing them.

Joys procured:
- To the *mind* by bright pleasant words.
- To the *heart* by a word of grateful love.
- To the *soul* by a word of heaven.

III.

FOR MY SOUL

Courage.
- In contradictions and trials:
  - Disturbances,
  - Sickness,
  - Failures,
  - Humiliations.
- In the causeless ennui which takes possession of me;
- In the ill-humor which arises in me, that it may never make others suffer;
- In my falls that I may quickly rise again;
- In my temptations that I may calmly repel them.

Order and regularity.
- In my occupations—each one in its hour;
- In my recreations;
- In the material objects which are for my use;
- To avoid stiffness and constraint, as well as caprice and fancies.

Nourishment.
- Pious thoughts read, reflected upon, sometimes written;
- Strengthening, elevating reading, exciting a love for the good and beautiful;
- Conversations which reanimate, rejoice, and even rejuvenate;
- Walks which relax and freshen the mind while strengthening the body.

XXIII.

THE DEMONS OF THE HEARTH.

Ennui.

Ennui is one of the most dangerous *demons of the hearth.*

It rarely attacks a *child;* it contents itself with hovering from time to time about a young girl to make its entrance into her soul; it establishes itself in the soul of a worldly woman who has never known true piety or with whom only its perfume remains.

***

Ennui begins by softly gliding into the heart in an unoccupied hour; it smiles upon it, flatters it, rocks it in soft and idle reveries; hence it captivates the *imagination*, then it seizes the *soul* which it causes to sleep.

And once the poor soul sleeps it ceases to pray, to labor; its imagination and heart lead it first *far from* duty, then *far from* God, so far sometimes that it can hardly find the path to return.

These are not attractive, romantic pages on ennui which we are about to collect, but a clear and precise picture of it.

Ennui would willingly smile upon and gladly flatter itself with gracious words depicting its state of languor.

I.

What Ennui is.

Ennui is a state which furnishes the *imagination* no element to fix it.

To the *mind* no useful and fruitful thought.

To *desires* no object.

To the *soul* no mission.

To the *heart* no avowable affection.

In this state everything displeases, wearies and fatigues one.

One's family is only a prison, the affection of a mother only a constraint, the sweet affection of a sister or a friend only an encumbrance, labor only a too heavy burden, devotion only a poetical word.

II.

What Ennui Leads to.

Ennui leads to sin, and particularly to a habit of sin.

To dryness of heart.

To enervation of soul.

To a waste of all the faculties.

Ennui permits all things, excuses all things, justifies all things.

Ennui ages one interiorly and exteriorly.

III.

What Ennui Supposes.

Ennui supposes:

1. *That we have no grief.* Grief occupies us, fills us, absorbs us; in grief we

weep, we suffer, we are desolate, but *we are not ennuyé.*

2. *That we have too much material welfare.* When daily need spurs us we exert ourselves, we contrive, we weary ourselves, particularly when we have some one about us whom we love and who suffers; but *we do not experience ennui.*

Moral welfare produces ennui as well. We are surrounded by those who flatter us, love us, care for us; we receive much and give nothing; and the heart withers under this shower of roses.

In short, *we are too happy.*

Oh, how a slight but telling trial, such as a brusque and unexpected separation from one of those to whom our heart is accustomed, and whom, after all, we really love, would give to the soul the energy it lacks!

"My God," said a Christian who feared ennui because she knew it unconsciously leads to perdition, "*My God, do not leave me a day without some spur.*"

IV.

How Ennui is Cured.

The remedy is infallible. It is easy, it is sweet to the heart, it is pleasing to the imagination; it needs but a *generous effort*.

Rouse yourself, heart given over to ennui!

***

You have no real grief, but there are griefs about you consuming the heart and soul of one you love; the soul and heart of your father and your mother perhaps; take upon yourself the mission to heal them; you can do it.

Grief is a *malady* which can be *alleviated* by loving and sympathetic words, which can be *healed* by delicate attentions, by patient hearing, and by continued devotion. Become the physician of souls and hearts; you will see how the bloom will come back to your life.

***

You have no grave sorrow; take upon yourself the sorrow of another.

Do you know the name of these sorrows? They are called, *hunger*, which tortures, *misery* and *abandonment*, which lead to blasphemy and depravity, *dishonor*, which leads, sometimes, to suicide.

O you who are rich, have you never heard in the depth of your soul the wail of distress? Was it the cry of a child, of an old man, of an unhappy motherless girl?

Rouse yourself then, do not be satisfied with sending an alms! Go, letting your heart guide you, become the *providence* of the unfortunate, and you will see how your life will bloom again.

XXIV.

LITTLE DEVICES FOR RESTORING PEACE TO THE SOUL, AND CAUSING IT TO ACQUIRE MERIT.

Receive graciously all who come to us, and never let them go away without consolation and peace.

How little it would cost us to do this, how good, and above all, how meritorious and sanctifying it would be!

Thus would Jesus do were He upon earth; and was it not thus He did? Who among the *poor*, the *unfortunate*, the *sick*, the *guilty*, or among those who *besought* Him did He ever repel, or permit to believe that their presence wearied Him?

The person who comes to me to be comforted or strengthened is frequently sent *directly* by God, who inspired her to come to me rather than to another. If God had not willed it would she have thought of me? Would He not have arrested her steps?

This person who comes to me is always accompanied by God, who *wishes to see if I shall be kind*, and who bears for me a special grace to help me *to do what He Himself would do, and also to enable me to acquire something for heaven.*

***

No, certainly, Jesus would not always have given material alms on earth. There were times when He would have been unable to do so; but He would have always peacefully received souls, He would have patiently heard them, He would have answered with kindness, He would have spoken with simplicity.

His words, His bearing, His glance, His lips would have radiated charity, compassion, joy.

And the person who is now with me, who involuntarily inconveniences me, who wearies me perhaps by her slowness or her importunity, would have come from Him happier, and above all, holier.

***

Oh, if Jesus received in the morning's Communion dwells in us by His grace, and if we are careful to live in the presence of God, how readily He will choose us to take His *place* with souls; what charm He will give us to attract, what peace, sweetness, joy, serenity, and strength He will give us for others, at the same time permitting us the enjoyment of these gifts ourselves.

It is told of a Saint that each time any one came to him, or the steps of a visitor fell upon his ear, he distinctly heard his guardian angel say, *God is here, be kind!*

My God! my God! I dare not express my heart's desire, but Thou seest it, Thou who seest all things.

XXV.

THE FIAT OF A DESOLATE SOUL.

Into Thy hands, into Thy hands, O my God!

Turn, mould this clay, form it, then shatter it if Thou wilt; it is Thine, it must utter no word. It suffices me that it serves Thy designs for me, and that nothing in me resists Thy holy will.

Order, command, forbid!
What wilt Thou that I do?
Whither wilt Thou that I go?
Whither wilt Thou that I go not?

Creatures, instruments whom God uses to mould my soul, behold me, act, do all that He commands you, for I know that even without your knowledge you must needs do to me but what He wills.

Suffering, exalted, humbled, useful for something, useless in all things, I shall ever adore Thee, ever love Thee, O my God!

Solitary and unknown as the desert flower, wandering like a bird, with no nest where I may rest, the submissive words of Mary shall be ever on my lips, *Fiat, fiat! Be it done to me according to Thy word!*

XXVI.

APOSTLESHIP IN A FAMILY.

The Net.

We have mentioned the apostleship of affectionate, insinuating, delicate words; the apostleship of *suffering* and of *expiation*, continued as long as the sin endures. Here now is another apostleship, ingeniously called by the children who invented it, the *Apostleship of the Net!*

When you wish, a pious child writes us, to recapture a pet bird without alarming or hurting it, you cast about it a large net, which you gradually and gently draw in so that the bird is scarcely conscious of it until it is under your hand.

In like manner, if you would win back a soul to God without wounding or irritating it, cast about it a *net* of *prayers*, which will extend over its every hour and moment if possible.

For this there should be several persons—three, five, ten; the more numerous they are the closer the *mesh of the net*, and the sooner is the soul captured.

Each of the members who compose the net choose a half hour, or quarter of an hour, resolving that each time the clock strikes they will offer a certain *little invocation* for this soul.

Each member takes *her half hour apart*, or decides to say her prayers every half hour, or every quarter of an hour, so that from every corner of the house, every half hour of the day the good God hears some such appeal as the following: *My God, bring back to Thee the soul of——! My God, incline my brother's heart to keep Thy ways.*

This invocation is made quite softly, sometimes in the presence of him for whom we are praying, and who is wholly unconscious of it, and then what bright smiles are exchanged at the sound of the clock, what pleasant words recalling the *wonderful net we are constructing!*

Dear children in the same family, dear souls united by the same spiritual tie in a community or in an association, cast about the soul whom you see has wandered from God your *net of little prayers;* continue it for a week, a month; then leave it for awhile, then begin again; the soul thus surrounded will struggle for a time, then it will feel itself captured, and you will see it slowly taking the path to the Church, where awaits him Jesus, the loving Father who sent you in search of him.

XXVII.

THE SAMARITAN'S BALM.

Do you know that popular remedy called *Samaritan's Balm*, which is used in maladies which *stiffen* the limbs?

This balm, inspired by a page of the

Gospel, is composed of *oil and wine;* it is inexpensive, easily prepared, and rubbed on aching limbs rarely fails to give relief.

⁎

A little oil and a little wine—a little kindness and a little courage, what a salutary balm this would be for the maladies of heart and soul which bring constraint into family relations.

A little *oil* and a little *wine* for this sinking heart which believes itself forgotten and despised, and which keeps itself apart. Oh, how quickly a mark of confidence, a little word of praise, would heal it!

A little *oil* and a little *wine* for this over sensitive, delicate heart which dare not labor more because it has made a mistake, or has pained us. Ah, an affectionate word and a kind greeting would make it draw near and give it new life.

For the maladies of heart and soul, all the science of books is not worth the mother's system caring herself for her child, *little attentions, anticipating wants, hope in God.*

***

Make a provision of smiles, of sweet words, of *encouragement and praise,* you who have the mission to lead souls to heaven.

XXVIII.

PROVISIONS OF THE SOUL.

Pray, Pray Always.

Sweet words which fell from the lips of Jesus, it is of you that I to-day seek *provision for my soul,* for the portion of the year which is now before me.

I need to pray!

I thirst for prayer!

I long to pray!

Oh, cause me to see all that is good, sweet, consoling, salutary in prayer!

And let the thoughts with which you inspire me, taking form and life, surround me, and captivate my imagination and my heart, each time duty or affection tells me I am to speak to God.

***

Each *word* of my prayer *slowly and piously uttered* makes reparation for a blasphemy.

Each *word* arrests a punishment, placing itself between God and the guilty soul.

Each *word* causes a special grace to fall from the heart of Jesus upon the soul of the dying, or upon a soul about to commit a mortal sin.

Each *word* alleviates the sufferings of a soul in Purgatory.

Each *word* gives a thrill of new joy to the Blessed Virgin always happy to see her Son loved, blessed, praised, glorified.

***

O my soul! O my soul! Would you **not pray well?**

Each *word* of my prayer *slowly and piously* uttered is a portion of that *coat of mail* which I weave about my soul, and which will protect it not from trials or temptations, but **from** wounds which weaken it and give it death.

Therefore, how strong I feel afterwards; and how fearlessly I undertake that hourly combat which I must wage against indolence, pride, cupidity, sensuality, selfishness, revolt.

**

Each *word* of my prayer *slowly and piously uttered* forms also the same *protecting mail* in which I may envelop the soul of those whom I love.

Oh, what joy to think that while I pray each of my words really forms a *buckler* for the soul of my father, my mother, my friend whom I know is exposed to temptation and trial, and who now will feel them less cruelly.

Each *word* is a drop of balm which I cause to fall upon a heart which I know is suffering, a heart which I have wounded perhaps, and from whom I dare not directly ask pardon?

Oh, after my prayer with what a calm and smiling countenance I may approach him. Have I not healed the wound I had caused him?

Each *word* of my prayer slowly and piously uttered is a *warm and soothing ray* which softly penetrates the heart of him with whom I have to treat of business.

I may calmly approach him; under the effect of the divine influence, which penetrates him without his knowledge, he will be just, he will be kind, he will be conciliating.

O my soul! O my soul! Wouldst thou not pray well?

Each *word* of my prayer *slowly* and piously uttered is a *piece* of *money* which my guardian angel bears to God in payment for my numerous faults; and the more frequent, pious, and recollected my prayer, the more I remit of my debt to God!

And after my death I shall see above near God all these *words* of my prayer as brilliant as pearls forming my immortal crown.

Each *word* of my prayer slowly and piously uttered is a mysterious fabric which in some way, I know not how, repairs the *breaches* in my past day, *binds* together again the hours which I had separated by a culpable loss of time, reunites two hearts which I had separated by an imprudent word.

Each *word* of my prayer *slowly and piously uttered* is a cry of love, a cry of hope, a cry of joy, a cry of distress, which pierces heaven, and I am sure that it is answered by another cry; the cry of Thy love, O my God!

Oh, you whose heart has been moved by the cry *My mother!* on the lips of a suffering or frightened child can form some idea of what passes in the heart of *your Father in heaven* when a desolate or loving soul cries, My God!

XXIX.

TO MAKE FRIENDS.

The possession of friends is the purest happiness and the greatest source of sweetness in life.

Having friends is multiplying one's life and one's knowledge. We are three, said a philosopher, but, as we have but one heart we see through the mind of all, we labor with the strength of all.

Having friends is strengthening one's heart against trial; it is giving it means of rising more easily to God.

A friend, says De Maistre, is a *conductor which carries off sorrow*. Nothing is so healing as the balm of affection.

But friends must be won. Being loved for one's self alone is a romantic dream. God makes advances to win friends, why should not we?

Character doubtless has much to do with friendship affording more or less sympathy, but *unselfish efforts* complete what sympathy has begun.

To have friends *merit them.* If you do not merit esteem and you have exterior qualities which please, or riches which dazzle, or a position which can afford protection—three things which attract time-servers—you will perhaps be flattered, you will not be loved.

* * *

Friendship is as delicate and *timid* as a dove. She must be approached softly, and allured gently; but once *taken* how *faithful* she is and how she fills all life with her grace and beauty.

Do you know what attracts her?

Good will and *affability*—obscure little virtues, one of which does not see or at least does not look at the defects of others, and the other, which attracts by a hidden charm pervading one's bearing, one's smile, one's words.

Little virtues which cost little and are of great value.

It is sometimes possible to be too kind; we never have too much good will and affability.

Kindness. There is nothing which more strongly attracts and binds a heart than deeds of kindness, and the heart which is insensible to them is a bad heart.

Kind deeds are the net which we must cast every hour; many hearts will doubtless escape; sufficient will remain to compensate you for the trouble you have taken and the outlay you have made.

Is not happiness worth a little fatigue? The basis of happiness is *kindness*.

Consideration. This is the *small coin* of kindness and affability; it is current everywhere, with all, and always brings back a little friendship.

The considerate man not only avoids giving pain, but he further enters into the tastes, the views of all, and profits by the least occasion to give pleasure.

Thus, you will find that I have spoken better than another who nevertheless shall have said the same thing. You do not grow weary in diverting my weariness; you study my humor to which you subject yours; you never wound my self-love by a too vivid picture of my faults; the duty which I have neglected you perform, leaving me to believe I have done it myself.

How could I not love you?

But consideration requires a good deal of tact. *Do too little*, you are rude—*do too much*, you are officious.

We must be considerate: *in heart* to love, *in mind and tact* to do fittingly what is to be done, *in patience* to long bear with forgetfulness and even *lack of gratitude*.

Let us try to gain a friend each day. Doubtless we may not always preserve them, but there will surely be among them an affectionate heart won by our kindness, and if one becomes an intimate friend of the soul, surely we are repaid.

Perhaps it is better to be able to say *my friend* than *my friends*.

An art still more difficult than making friends is the art of preserving them. We shall speak of this again elsewhere. Only remember that *the pleasures of friendship, the duties of friendship*, are synonymous terms to kind hearts.

Two words now, only two words to you friends whom piety has united in the same thoughts, in the same desires.

That your love may long endure in all its tenderness, *always live as if* you were on the eve of parting and desired to leave a mutually pleasant memory.

Then do *not judge your friend;* according as we begin to judge, our love begins to weaken.

∗
*

Would you finally be sure that you are loved and that you truly love? See if in your friend and yourself there are these four qualities.

Prudent liberty, which reproves in a friend the weaknesses he should correct, but does it with a tact and delicacy which never causes a friend to blush.

Frank and confiding intercourse, in which counsel is simply given and asked.

Courageous justice to undertake the defence of a friend in order to establish, increase, or maintain his reputation, even at the risk of personal unpleasantness.

Constant kindness, which is a support and consolation, making us always easy of access, and enabling our friend to count upon us always and in all things.

XXX.

LITTLE DEVICES FOR RESTORING PEACE TO THE SOUL AND CAUSING IT TO ACQUIRE MERIT.

Not to Complain too much, but Keep for a Time in the Depth of the Soul the Trial God has sent.

It is doubtless a relief to complain, but the relief is only momentary, and complaining really cures nothing.

Complaints importune others.

Complaints aggravate the temper of him who makes them, increase the trouble of his soul, irritate his mind and his heart.

Complaints are rarely without sin, for they exaggerate the faults of those who have wounded us.

Complaints above all prevent the trials from having upon the soul the *sanctifying effect* for which God permitted them.

Oh, if we knew how to keep, only for a few hours, in silence and peace that disagreeable word which wounded us, that calumny or that suspicion which God has sent to cure the *pride*, the *jealousy*, the *sensuality* which mar and consume our souls, what salutary remedies they would prove!

Will we not remain motionless entire days in order not to disarrange an uncomfortable bandage or apparatus which is to restore an injured member?

Do we not submit to solitude, privation, inconvenience to leave a remedy time to reach the seat of disorder and produce its effect?

Oh, how many would be saints if they had allowed the *remedies sent by God* time to produce their effect.

You instantly reject that humiliation, you struggle against a circumstance which tries you, *the remedy is wasted, the cure has to be begun again.*

* *
*

Every trial, whether *failure, calumny, malice, injustice, sickness, solitude, neglect,* is really a *remedy* which God applies or causes to be applied to us to cure our sick soul, to prevent a grave malady, to save us from a serious fault into which we were about to fall.

God like earthly physicians has remedies which are *curative,* and remedies which are *preservative.* He acts upon us by means of creatures which are His own *instruments*—but we may be sure that the instruments are used by a *practised* and *above all* a *fatherly hand.*

₊₊*

It may be a superior, a confessor, an intimate friend, an acquaintance, a stranger who has wounded us. Poor soul writhing under the sting of injustice and calumny, do you think the person who is the cause of your suffering acted without God's *knowledge*—without God *willing it*—without God *measuring how far the cruel, calumniating, unjust words would penetrate your soul, your heart, your reputation*—without God *watching with fatherly care the depth of the wound you received, and without His placing in it a grace which would prevent it from becoming angry and inflamed?*

Oh, how little Christian we are, my God!

How little we trust Thee, my God!

What! I abandon often to an unknown physician my most delicate members that he may operate upon them; he pierces my flesh, he causes the blood to flow, and in the midst of my tears I *thank him and I pay him;* and Thou my God, Thou my Father, Thou whose kindness is *beyond anything that it is possible to imagine,* when Thou dost pierce my soul to extricate the pride which would destroy it, when Thou dost rend my heart to wrest from it an affection which would stain it, I murmur, I cry, I complain, I seek to break the instrument of Thy hand, as if Thou wert not free to use as an *instrument whomsoever Thou choosest!*

Pardon, O my God, pardon!

But must we never complain, then, must we never speak of our trials? And do we not need a word from a friend, *a human word* to strengthen us, to raise us up, to encourage us?

Does not God wish that I should mingle my tears with those of my friend? That I should seek from him a word of sympathy, of consolation and love?

Has not God made friendship? And of what avail is friendship if it does not console us?

I understand this cry of the heart! Yes, yes, God has made friendship and He has made it compassionate.

Go then to your friend, but go first to that other friend Jesus in the Eucharist. Give the trial time to produce its divine effect upon your soul. Accept it, give thanks for it, embrace it, say peacefully and lovingly: *Yes, my God, yes,*

Thou hast done wisely to send me this trial, this fear which troubles me a little, this deception which humiliates me—I accept it, I wish it, I *embrace it.*

Then go to your friend, and he will say to you the words which Jesus has not audibly spoken to you.

And when you shall have relieved your heart by that sweet outpouring of holy friendship, you will calmly and peacefully take up life's duties again and await without bitterness the end of your trial.

XXXI.

THE HOLY SHADOW.

A long time ago there lived a saint so good that the angels astonished at his holiness came expressly from heaven to see how any one on earth could so closely resemble the good God.

And he kept simply on his way spreading the example of virtue as naturally as the stars shed light and the flowers give perfume.

Two words summed up his day—he *gave* and *forgave;* but these words were never on his lips; you read them in his smile, in his amiability, in his complaisance, in his untiring charity.

The angels said to God, "Lord, grant him the gift of miracles."

"Willingly," replied the good God, "ask him what he wishes."

And the angels said to the saint, "Wouldst thou have the gift of healing, so that when thy hands touch an infirm body it shall be made whole?"

"No," replied the saint, "I would rather the good God did it Himself."

"Wouldst thou have thy words win back guilty souls and erring hearts to God?"

"No, that is the mission of the angels and unfit for a poor creature like me. I pray, I do not work conversions."

"Wouldst thou be a model of patience,

attracting souls to thee by the splendor of thy virtues, and thus glorify God?"

"No," replied the saint, "if they were attached to me they would be estranged from God. The good God has many other means of causing His name to be glorified."

Finally the angels said, "What will you have?"

And the saint smiled and said, "What can I ask? That God may leave me His grace; with it do I not possess all things?"

The angels insisted saying: "Nevertheless you must ask a miracle, or we will forcibly impose one upon you."

"Then let me do a great deal of good without ever knowing it," said the saint.

The angels consulted together for some time how this could be accomplished; then they asked the good God to grant that every time the saint's shadow fell at either side or behind him so that he could not see it, it should have the power of curing the sick, consoling the afflicted, and comforting the sorrowful.

Our Lord assented.

And wherever the saint's shadow fell thus the pathways bloomed, the parched earth was refreshed, the turbid streams became pure and limpid, the dying flowers revived, a fresh healthy bloom came to the pale cheeks of little children, and tears of joy to the eyes of sorrowing mothers.

But the saint kept simply on his way, unconsciously spreading the example of his virtues as naturally as the stars shed light, as the flowers give perfume. And the people respecting his modesty followed him in silence, never speaking to him of his miracles. They gradually forgot even his name, and simply called him "*The Holy Shadow.*"

XXXII.

USELESS.

A biographer in the life of a saint wrote these lines, *He labored thirty years to render himself useless.*

The proof-reader, believing it a mistake of the author, rewrote it, *He labored thirty years to render himself useful.*

The reader did not accept it in the *Christian sense.*

Doubtless the labor of the Christian soul should be *useful;* but she should *labor hidden in her work and disappear.* She should regard herself as but *an instrument* which has the mission to turn to account the skill of the master, an *instrument* which is to be worn out in labor, then left and forever forgotten.

O my soul! behold what you are: *an instrument of God*, but an instrument which feels, which desires, which loves. Behold your mission: to hide yourself under the divine Hand which employs you, in order that *only* the *Hand* and the *work* it does through you shall be visible.

Labor then directed by the hand of this divine Master, and when you shall be worn out and the Master lets you fall to take another younger, stronger, more apt than you, *quietly retire and disappear without murmur to be unknown and forgotten.*

Are you not happy to have served God?

Oh! if the pen, the instrument of the loving heart of St. Francis of Sales, had life as I have, how it would have thanked him for having used it and worn it out writing those beautiful pages of the *Treatise on the Love of God.*

Enviable pen, what has become of thee? Who knows thee? Who thinks of thee?

But I know that Thou my God, Thou wilt be ever mindful of Thy little instrument, particularly when she shall have become worn and completely useless in Thy service! Oh, grant me to be forgotten, unknown by all and loved by Thee alone, my God!

XXXIII.

WHAT THE SMILE OF A SAINT SAYS.

A friend offered me yesterday an engraving of the portrait of St. Francis of Sales.

The saint was represented with a pen in his hand, but the pen was motionless, it appeared to be waiting or rather resting, it seemed to me as though St. Francis wished to speak.

His clear frank eyes looked sweetly down upon me and easily followed my every movement.

His brow shone with a heavenly light and on his lips was a peaceful smile, the result of goodness, peace, purity and strength; his sweet parted lips seemed to be murmuring a few words.

O holy Saint! O my dear Saint, speak, speak to me, I cried. And I seemed to hear the following words which I gathered as precious pearls which I wish to piously re-read every day:

I made myself little to lead the little ones; and like the good Shepherd I measured my steps to those of my little lambs; doubtless I led them on, but I did not urge them too much for fear of wearying them.

**

I received every one graciously, and sent no one away whatever his condition. I peacefully heard every one, and as long as he wished, as if I had but that to do. Was not each one's guardian angel present to watch and study me?

**

I was very yielding to the wishes of others, seeking not to make them go with me, but endeavoring to go with them. Oh how good it is and what a source of peace it is to be thus yielding to the wishes of others and easily fitted to any purpose!

*_**

I looked upon this life as a journey which we have to make united to those whom God places with us along the way, and these companions of the way I willingly accepted. God sent them to me and I bore with them, helped them and loved them. When they reach the end of the journey must they not be able to tell God that I have been kind to them?

*_**

I never was angry but once in my life, and I have always regretted it.

*_**

I have always been like the good Samaritan, who could not pass a sufferer without stopping to console him, and I have always poured oil and wine on the wound of a suffering soul. My God, if I must err in any extreme, let it be that of gentleness!

*_**

Let God treat me as He will, it is all one to me provided I serve Him. These are marvellous words, therefore I pondered over them, and turned them over in my mind, letting them softly melt in my mouth. If you knew the peaceful content they left in my soul.

There is no one in the world who feels *trials of the heart* more keenly than I; nevertheless I make so little account of life here below, that I never turn to God with more love than when He has afflicted me or caused me to be afflicted. Then my heart is like the trees from which balm is extracted: the more they are pierced and rent the greater perfume they shed about them. The more I was grieved the more I loved.

Sweetly and gently: I would have these two words written on my every action, my every word.

Little and good, little and sweet, little and constant; I exacted no more of myself nor of others.

XXXIV

THE POWER OF AN ACT OF LOVE OF GOD.

Have you ever reflected on the power of *an act of love of God?*

Let us recall first the simple words of which it is composed:

O my God! I love Thee above all things with my whole heart and soul, with all my strength, because Thou art infinitely good!

Try to utter these words slowly that each one may sink into your soul.

Do you not feel that you are sensibly moved and that your whole being goes out with those words to God, to enter in a certain sense into His being and to give Him your whole life?

Do you not feel that in making this act you give more than if you gave your riches, your strength, your time, or rather that this act of love bears *you* with it and *gives you with your riches, your strength, your time, all that you possess to God?*

Imagine that a child was now before you, a child who had grievously offended you, if you wish, but whose sincerity you cannot doubt, who, impelled neither by fear nor interest, but only by his repentant heart, comes to you and addresses you in the words of this act, would it have no effect upon you? Would it excite in you no tender fatherly feeling?

I defy you to remain unmoved and not to feel your arms involuntarily extend to embrace the poor child while your lips murmur, *I also love thee!*

Another thing which is impossible to you, to you desolate, guilty, despairing souls who see within you and about you but *fear, terror* and—horrible word! —damnation. I defy you to go before a crucifix or before the Tabernacle and say to Jesus, dwelling upon each of the words in proportion to the resistance you feel in uttering them: *My God, I love Thee above all things with my whole heart and soul with all my strength, because I know and I feel that Thou art good, infinitely good,* and not feel that Jesus is moved, and not hear Jesus say, *I also love you.*

Do not reason. Try, try, or else acknowledge this horrible thought, *that He does not know what it is to love, or His heart is less kind than yours!*

O Jesus, how shall I find words to express the love awakened in Thee by a tender word from the heart of one of Thy poor children on earth? In Thy heart, so delicate, so tender, so sensitive so loving!

Father Faber uses an expression which seems strange to us who are so little supernatural: *God,* he says, *seems to court our love,* that He in His turn may not only love us, for he always loves us, but that He may make us feel that He loves us.

Acts of love require hardly a few seconds. All day long, even in the midst of our labor, we may multiply these acts almost infinitely; and see what marvels they effect!

The heart of Jesus is really moved to happiness, and sheds more abundant graces upon the earth.

It thrills the Blessed Virgin, increases her love for us, and, if it were possible, we should hear tender words of thanks from her lips.

Our guardian angel, much moved, draws nearer to us, as if to make us feel that we are good.

The angels who people the air experience a thrill of joy, and look upon us with ineffable tenderness.

The demons feel their power weakened, and there is a truce in the temptations with which they overwhelm men.

The choirs of the blessed in heaven redouble their hymns of joy.

All souls on earth experience something of its divine influence.

An act of love from the heart of a poor sick man, of a poor, perhaps despised, servant, thus moves the whole world.

**

Oh, who would not multiply *acts of love of God* during the day?

At this moment, at least, you who read these lines, *souls* united by the reading of *Golden Sands*, pause for an instant, and say from the depths of your heart, *My God, I love Thee! My God, I love Thee!*

XXXV.

WINGS.

Wings! Wings! Who has not more than once sent from his soul this cry of sadness, of hope, of love?

Who has not longed to give wings to his soul, that it might leave the narrow realities of earth and rise to the infinite?

The infinite with us is not the *vague reverie* of the dreamer; the infinite is Thee, my God! Thee our refuge in trouble; Thee our strength in weakness; Thee our love in abandonment!

Wings! Wings! My heart would rise! I know that God binds me to duty, and that I must bend under the weight of labor, sorrow, separation, contempt sometimes, until the hour of my recall; but I would I had wings to rise and renew my energy and my will above, near Thee, my God!

Wings! Wings! Is it not the cry of the Church, who every day and hour in the Holy Sacrifice repeats, by the lips of her priests, *Sursum corda?*

***

Children, continue in peace at your

family hearth, continue to work at your mother's side, occupying your hands with the labors of the household but let us, oh, let us sometimes point out to you heaven, and bear your souls thither! To raise one's soul is to strengthen one's heart.

These lines which we reproduce below are for you, and were written by a young girl whose name we regret not to know.

Do not fear the enthusiasm they may awaken in your soul. Enthusiasm draws us to God.

WINGS.

Would I had wings in ecstasy to rise
    Above this world of bitterness, and flee
Beyond the splendor of the changeful skies,
    Nearer, my God, oh, nearer still to Thee!

To pass the flaming border, and to drown
    My heart in bliss ineffable above;
To see the cradle of my soul, and crown
    Its exiled hopes with God's unchanging love

Would I had wings to hasten my farewell
   To earth, its death, its tempests, and its tears;
To see my mother's God, and simply tell
   To Him the story of my childhood's years;

To pass forever from the earth, and part
   With earthly woe forever, and to rest
Where sorrow lives not and the wearied heart
   May find repose eternal in His breast.

Would I had wings to see again the dead,
   The dear ones dead, whom God has called before,
To that dear land where all my hopes have fled,
   To bloom forever on the golden shore.

For wings to fly where never yet was strife,
   Where tempests sleep and silent is their breath
Beyond, above the very bounds of life;
   Above, beyond the cruel grasp of death.

Wings for my heart, wings for my soul, I pray!
   They weary of their exile long and drear;
They seek the splendor of the endless day.
   Thou callest them, O God! they hear, they hear.

Des ailes! pour voler jusqu'au palais des anges
   Dans l'infini, partout, dans le firmament bleu!
Des ailes! pour quitter ce monde plein de fange.
   Des ailes! pour voler plus près de vous mon Dieu!

Des ailes! pour voler aux horizons de flammes
   De célestes amours désaltérer nos cœurs!
Des ailes! pour revoir le berceau de nos âmes,
   Vague et cher souvenir d'ineffable bonheur!

Des ailes! pour voler bien loin de notre terre,
   Loin du deuil, de la mort, loin des noirs ouragans!
Des ailes pour porter mes pleurs et ma prière
   Au bon Dieu de ma mère et des petits enfants.

Des ailes! pour quitter nos misères profondes!
   Des ailes! pour aller où finit la douleur!
Des ailes! pour aller au-delà de nos mondes!
   Des ailes! pour savoir où poser notre cœur!

Des ailes! pour voler vers l'étendue immense
   Où déjà sont montés tant de morts bien-aimés!
Des ailes! pour voler où s'enfuit l'espérance,
   Où germent les bonheurs sur la terre semés!

Des ailes! pour aller à la plage bénie,
   Où pour jamais enfin la tempête s'endort;
Des ailes! pour voler au-dessus de la vie!
   Des ailes! pour voler au-delà de la mort!

Des ailes! pour mon cœur, des ailes pour mon âme
   Captifs impatients de l'extase éternel!
Des ailes! pour aller où le jour prend sa flamme.
   Des ailes! pour voler, Seigneur, à votre appel!

XXXVI.

BE SERIOUS.

A statesman who had retired from public life, and devoted his last days to *serious thoughts*, was visited by some friends, who taxed him with having become *melancholy*.

No, he replied, I am only *serious*. Everything about me is serious, and, for the peace of heart and soul, I feel the necessity of being in unison with my surroundings.

See, he added, with a gravity which impressed those present, God is *serious* when He observes us, Jesus is *serious* when He intercedes for us, the Holy Spirit within us is *serious* when He counsels us, the demon is *serious* when he tempts us, the reprobates in the torments of hell are *serious*, for not having been so on earth—everything is *serious* in the country to which we are going. O my friends, my friends, believe me! Let us, from time to time at least, be *serious*, in the thoughts of our minds, in the projects of our hearts.

XXXVII.

A CHILD OF MARY'S LIFE.

Nothing renders life sweeter, more useful, more meritorious than to live in the presence of God, under the protection of His Mother, finding in each hour a duty, and gently devoting all our energies to its perfect accomplishment.

Nothing, particularly, better prepares us for the shocks which from time to time disturb the sweet and peaceful monotony of our firesides.

Alas! young girls, so full of illusions, and so sweetly flattered by the hope of a life ever increasing in beauty, you must expect these *trials*.

In vain does your imagination clothe

in beauty the path which opens before you; in vain do tenderness, devotion, friendship remove from it all that could mar its brilliancy. The path of life is like a railway—the train—upon its iron track speeds smoothly for many miles, encountering no obstacle, when suddenly a little stone, coming we know not whence, suffices to throw it from the rails and occasion a terrible catastrophe.

In life's pathway, when the heart remains in its place under the protection of God and duty, it is never turned from its path, but it must always expect to experience *severe shocks.*

It is to weaken these *shocks*, always very violent, that we offer you, dear Children of Mary, these counsels, which will surround you with peace, resignation, charity.

We do not promise you exemption from sorrow, deep grief, nor suffering under all its forms, but we promise you, if you daily read these lines and practise what they teach, we promise you *strength, light, merit,* particularly for heaven.

A CHILD OF MARY SHOULD BE

Occupied in prayer, charity, labor, union with God.

Charity she can always practise by a kind word, a smile, a friendly greeting, an alms.

Labor she can always find; let her hands never remain idle, let not her mind indulge in dreams.

Union with God is the fruit of prayer, of charity, of labor.

∗
∗ ∗

Free from dissipating thoughts, disquieting desires, disturbing projects.

Dissipating *thoughts* are those which divert her from labor and prayer.

Disquieting *desires* are those which she dare not confide to her mother.

Restless projects are those which leave the soul in idle reverie.

∗
∗ ∗

Mortified in her senses, in her inclinations, in her humor, in her disposition, and at all times granting to her senses only what is permissible, allowing to her humor and disposition nothing which could give pain to others.

*_{*}

Careful to irritate, to wound no one, to think ill, or speak ill of no one.

*_{*}

Modest in her dress, her bearing, her words, her carriage, and free from constraint, affectation, or singularity.

*_{*}

Patient in sickness, trials, contradictions, little crosses of every hour. How this daily patience will help her to be mistress of herself, to be cheerful and smiling, and particularly to stifle all murmurs.

Compassionate toward the wants of all; their sickness, their fatigue, their faults, even their whims.

*_{*}

Disinterested, seeking the glory of God, the salvation of all, the welfare of each member of the family, even at the expense of her own. She is never so happy as when she has *deprived* herself of something to give pleasure to her mother or sisters. How good it is to deny ourselves to give to others!

*_{*}

Disposed to suffer everything, to do everything, to pardon, to forget everything.

Devoted to her mother, whom she obeys in all things, whose wishes she endeavors to anticipate in all things; *devoted* to her sisters, whom she helps with her counsels, with her labor, to whom she gives all the time that can be useful to them; *devoted* to the labor imposed upon her, which she cheerfully and carefully performs.

Zealous to prevent wrong, to repair it, to make it forgotten; to give good example by her words, her prayers, her affability; seeking to win others only to lead them to God.

Hidden, loving to labor humbly and modestly under the eyes of God alone; finding herself happy in her room, at the foot of the tabernacle of Jesus, before the altar of Mary, her good and tender Mother. Humble, without affectation, with a humility which consists more in feeling than in words, gratefully accepting all the kindness she meets, never murmuring against an act of neglect or ill-will.

Peaceful, finally, and joyful, satisfied to be here where God wishes her, to do what God wills, desiring only what God wills, desiring neither more health nor fortune nor relations. She accepts all as coming from God, and convinced that she will never be abandoned by God, she leaves to Him the care of her future, sure that He prepares the *place* she is to occupy; and she waits without anxiety, firmly resolved to go generously wherever God shall call her.

XXXVIII.

AN UNKNOWN JOY.

A joy very sweet to the soul, a joy but little known — is to associate in thought *all whom we love* with what moves us, charms us, or enhances life. Alone in my cell I read something which captivates my mind, enlarges and elevates my soul, and causes it to experience that heavenly influence which cannot be expressed. In thought I assemble all my loved ones. Why should I enjoy it alone?

They are about me, present with me,

and then *I read more slowly,* as if they heard me, and I reread the page to make them relish the beauty which charms me.

And I close the book happier.

And so it is with all great, elevating, beautiful things. The soul relishes them less if she is alone; thus for her happiness she peoples her solitude; peoples it with her *dear absent ones,* taken from her by death or by estrangment; she no longer sighs for their presence, but really feels they are with her.

Is bodily presence then necessary, that souls may see and converse together?

And when my thought rises above these loved ones, and, becoming more enlightened, calls upon Thee, my God! *it is God who deigns to come,* God who makes me feel His presence as the intimate friend, the smiling companion of my solitude.

And this beautiful, this attractive

book I *read* to God, who hears me, who seems to me to enjoy it with me, and *thanks* me.

This letter which I have received *we read together*, God and I; God expounds it, explains it; He softens such a word which could irritate me; He fills another with a peace, a strength, a consolation which I never should have found.

This page which I write under His dictation *I read to God;* He corrects it, He blesses it, He renders it fruitful, and I thank Him.

And from time to time I rest in silence; I see nothing, but I know that I am not alone, and that I am loved; I hear nothing, but I know that something is said to me.

Is it necessary to see one another to love, is it necessary to speak to understand one another?

And when the hour of a duty comes and interrupts this *twofold converse*, the separation, which is only momentary, leaves no trouble after it.

It leaves a shade of sadness, but we softly whisper, *Till this evening! Till to-morrow!*

Oh, how they are to be pitied, those souls who know not how to live a few moments every day with their absent ones!

How they are to be pitied, those souls who must needs see and understand to feel happy!

XXXIX.

CONSOLATION.

You torment yourself, poor heart, that among the persons who surround you, with whom perhaps you are charged, there are *one* or two, even more, who cause you weariness. They do not like you, they find fault with all you do, they always meet you with a severe expression or an almost disdainful smile, they injure you, you say; they are at least an obstacle, you think, to the good you could do. And your life flows sad and discolored, and discouragement gradually penetrates your soul.

Courage! instead of being troubled, thank God. *These persons preserve your soul from humiliating faults, and perhaps grave falls.*

For you they are like the devices of medicine, intended to relieve the body gradually of a variety of injurious humors.

God, whose glance penetrates beyond the present hour, sees that *too much affection* would gradually enervate you, that you would attach yourself with a too human love, and, to preserve all the delicacy of your heart, He places about it thorns.

God sees that *too much joy,* and too much of that *comfort* resulting from those little attentions for which you yearn, would make you slothful in prayer, and He cuts you off from even what seems to you well merited. God sees that *too much flattery* would intoxicate you, and make you less kind to others, and He causes you to feel a few humiliations.

Then leave these persons to do their will; unconsciously to themselves they are doing God's work in you. Love them by *an effort of your will,* since you cannot love them through natural sympathy, and sometimes say to God, *My God, may their conduct, free from any offence against Thee, sanctify me; I need them.*

XL.

A CHARMING MEANS OF BEING KIND AND SECURING HAPPINESS.

It is the history of a friend which I wish to tell you; of a friend whom I should like to resemble because I would be as useful to others as he is to me, others would love me as I love him and then I should be happy.

He said to me only yesterday, *To be loved a little, to feel that one is of some little use, how pleasant it makes life!*

I.

We were together in a large studio where was a collection of treasures of industry and art.

Young men with obliging amiability showed us all these marvels and answered all our questions, reminding us of the happy times when kindly genii placed themselves at the service of men.

A sudden thought lit up the countenance of my friend. Oh, if in my little sphere, said he, I could be for those about me what these obliging men are to us!

If I could amass sufficient knowledge, so that those who have need of *counsel*, of *light*, *of strength*, would come to me! He paused for a moment. It requires but two things, he added, *labor and devotion*.

These two things I feel I possess, one in my *mind*, the other in my *heart*.

Well, I shall be *learned*, and *devoted*.

And he set to work, utilizing every moment.

Like the bee drinking the dew from every flower, seeking the history and the teaching of all that he encountered, noting, copying, writing, letting nothing escape his memory.

It is my *store-house*, he used to say; things are rather heaped together there, but when a *client* comes, I have an intelligent agent who quickly finds all that I am asked for.

Who is this agent?

My heart.

II.

This precious friend is *ambitious* for knowledge, he would know all things, and God smiles upon this ambition, because if He seeks to *know all things*, it is that he may communicate to others a knowledge which is easier gathered from his lips than learned from books.

If he searches the past, and patiently unravels obscure questions, it is to afford others a knowledge which they would only have acquired by weary labor.

He said to me one day, *I should like to be a dictionary, and within the reach of all, so that every one could run over the pages at their ease.*

And it is wonderful how the paternal hand of

God places under his eyes all that he needs. A *book* in an obscure corner of a neglected room, in books a *thought* which has never yet impressed any mind, in conversation a *word* which becomes for him a fruitful source of salutary and useful ideas.

If God wishes to make my mind a field, where His children may come to glean, must He not help me to fill it?

If God wishes to make me a hive, must He not cause me to discover honey?

And what a delightful hive indeed his memory is; what sweet, gentle words flow from his lips in answer to the least question, even of a child!

And his answers have not the dryness of the scholar seeking to convince you of *his own learning;* they are as simple as the words of a mother to her little one in the nursery; they softly penetrate and easily engrave themselves upon even the least attentive soul.

You never leave him without a desire to return.

His memory does not vanish like the perfume of the flowers; it remains in the soul like the harvest of the gleaner, like the honey which is gathered and laid by for time of need.

It is not merely that his answers are brilliant,

they are also *earnest* and communicate this earnestness to all souls.

It can be truly said of him, *He puts his whole heart into everything he says and does.*

III.

And his room? It is a little encumbered like his memory: *books, pictures, papers, and children's toys*—everything abounds there in such order perhaps as would not satisfy the director of a museum, but which is yet sufficient to enable him to find his way.

You would smile on entering, for every object seems as though it bore written upon it the pleasant words, For *myself and my friends.*

Yes, everything belongs to you who go to see him just as much as it does to him; one would say he was not the *owner*, only the *guardian*.

Come at what hour you will, *his room*, *his memory*, *his heart* are open to you. Those who enter, bring they never so little simplicity, are at their ease at once; they are made to feel they *are at home*.

One day when I smilingly remarked this to him, he said with simplicity, *But is it not the same when we go to see the good God?*

Good and amiable friend, what then is your secret of being so kind and giving so much happiness?

It is not you who will tell me, you do not know, perhaps; but your guardian angel will say:

He possesses God in the depth of his soul, and he preserves his soul pure and transparent, so that the rays God sheds abroad are not obscured, and it is God who attracts, God who speaks and teaches through him. He is only the good God's instrument.

XLI.

THE COMMUNION WHICH SANCTIFIES THE SOUL.

The fruit of a good communion *within* is fear of sin, *without*, kindness to others.

Communion is of itself *sanctifying*.

It introduces Jesus Christ into the soul, and Jesus who unceasingly *operates* always sheds grace about Him, as the sun always sheds its light, as fire always diffuses its heat.

It is impossible for even the simple

passage of Jesus Christ in a soul not to leave in it *something* of *Jesus Christ.*

But it is necessary that the soul be *prepared.* The fire, which of its nature is heating, only produces this effect in proportion as the body placed near it is capable of being easily penetrated by heat.

Does not this simple reflection explain the little effect produced by our frequent communions?

_

Do you wish then, O my soul, to receive in each communion that *something* which radiates from Jesus Christ, and which gradually shall make of you a creature wholly of heaven?

Do you wish, in receiving the *God of peace*, to have for those with whom you live words which, gently falling from your lips upon their souls, shall give them calmness, resignation, and peace?

Do you wish, in receiving the *God of love*, to feel your affection, your devotion, your tenderness gradually increasing and irresistibly impelling you to live for others, to serve them, to love them, in a word as Jesus would love them?

Do you wish, in receiving Him whom you so willingly call the *good God*, to become kind to endure, kind to compassionate, kind to pardon, and, in a measure, to take the place of this good God who gives Himself to you?

Then here is what you should be when you receive Holy Communion:

Resolved to fully observe the Commandments of God, not to hesitate when there is question of a duty to be performed however difficult, however severe it may appear, the duty of *pardoning and forgetting* an injustice or an unmerited humiliation, the duty of *accepting* a position which is contrary to your tastes, your abilities, the duty of *applying* yourself to a difficult perhaps obscure labor which breaks all your habits and seems above your strength.

And if a *duty* presents itself to you as *impossible* ask yourself simply, *Does God wish me to do it?* and if conscience answers *Yes*, then say, *I will do it.* After communion the *impossibility* will disappear.

*_**

Generous in sometimes denying yourself on the days of your communion those pleasures which have nothing positively wrong in them, but which you know by experience weaken your piety, excite your sensibility, and have an enervating effect upon you. We are not really generous unless we do a little more than *strict duty*.

Frank and straightforward in never stopping to consider whether something you are forbidden is a sin, and whether you cannot make a compromise between your conscience and the prohibition.

Oh, how the poor soul hesitating between God and the world, between duty and pleasure, between what is forbidden and what attracts, injures herself by this vacillation! Did Jesus Christ calculate the cost when He died for you? and you—you calculate, you measure your service! Cowardly soul!

Humble and modest, following peacefully in the path Providence opens before you, weeping sometimes perhaps, often suffering, but living without anxiety, peacefully awaiting the fatherly succor which never fails trusting souls who renew their strength in each communion, attracting little attention, loving neither the multitude nor applause, laboring for your maintenance if your condition requires it, doing good without seeking commendation or praise, tranquilly permitting others to live more honored, more esteemed, while your only ambition is to *love, to fervently love the good God, and be loved by Him.*

*_**

If you are thus disposed, O my soul, be sure that each communion will make you a little better, will cause you to resemble Jesus a little more, will give you a little more desire and relish for the things of God, and will avail you a new degree of glory for heaven.

Then do not hesitate to receive Holy Communion as frequently as you are permitted by the priest to whom God has confided you; perhaps you may still fall, but courage! Remember that *persevering* is not precisely exemption from falls, it is particularly *rising again.*

XLII.

One of the sweetest *flatteries*, the only one perhaps which the heart inspires and which will never cause a blush, is to let our friends believe *that they are indispensable to us, that we should be unhappy without them.*

There are hearts which so thirst to *give* and *devote themselves* that when once they find that where they have been accustomed to offer their devotion there is no longer place for *anything of them*, they go away seeking everywhere objects upon which to expend their kindness, almost entreating passers-by, *Let me give you something.* It is like the bee whose hive has been destroyed, and who suffers at not being able to give forth its honey. Oh, in pity for them let them, these old friends, believe that they are still useful to you, even though their labor may be a little of a burden to you!

XLIII.

A FEW MOMENTS BEFORE AN IMAGE OF THE BLESSED VIRGIN.

I.

Praise and Love.

HAIL MARY!

These are the words which when a little child, aided by my mother, I lisped before thy image, loving thee, O Mary, loving thee with all my heart even before I knew thee!

HAIL MARY!

Blessed words, which I have so often uttered since those early days, now so far distant, and which I again address to thee to-day.

O Mary! my soul has lost its candor of former days, but the more it advances in life, the more it feels thy power, thy love, thy mercy surrounding it, penetrating it, protecting its happiness; there are hours when my overcharged soul must pour out to thee its respect, its tenderness, its gratitude, its devotion to Jesus and to thee!

HAIL MARY!

What words recall sweeter memories to thy heart?

The memory of thy *simple fear* when the Angel, on the part of God, first saluted thee in these words.

The memory of *thy ardent love for purity*, which made thee so beautiful in the eyes of God.

The memory of thy *simple, frank, affectionate submission*, which drew the good God to thee.

The more touching memory of thy emotion when Jesus, thy Son, thy God, thy Creator, first saluted thee, saying, *Hail Mary!*

These are the memories I would awaken when I address thee: Hail Mary!—these are the thoughts I would recall to my soul to excite it to more respect, more tenderness, more gratitude, more devotion to Jesus and to thee!

HAIL MARY!

These are also the words of the poor mendicant, who before extending his hand endeavors to win the attention of the heart he seeks to move.

I am that poor mendicant, O Mary, and this *Hail Mary!* is to tell thee that here below on earth a soul implores thy aid, a suppliant holds out her hand to thee and begs of thee more respect, more tenderness, more devotion to Jesus and to thee.

FULL OF GRACE.

Grace is God's treasure, and God, who lavished this grace upon thee in thy *Immaculate Conception*, increased it in the *Incarnation* to an almost infinite degree, so that it is *thee* whom we must study to learn the riches of God, it is through thee we may ask them of God, it is through thy intercession that God enables us to attain them.

O Mary! what grand and magnificent riches the angels admire in thee!

Riches of mind. Thou hast *divine light*, which shines through thy pure soul like sunlight through crystal; and thou art the channel through which the Doctors of the Church receive from God the knowledge they impart to souls.

Thou art the seat and, as it were, the permanent abode of *divine wisdom*, and it is of thee that priests learn the counsels with which they lead souls to heaven.

It is always thee—always thy power with God, which the Church invokes when she is about to make one of her decisions which is to stand forever, always thee to whom she gives thanks when God has communicated to her the truths which nourish souls.

Riches of the heart. God has so abundantly endowed thee with goodness, tenderness, mercy, devotion, that mankind during countless ages unceasingly drawing from this merciful source graces of comfort, strength, and healing, could never even diminish the wealth of that heart which God has so abundantly filled.

And the soul knows no *bitterness* which thou canst not sweeten, no *sorrow* which thou canst not soothe, no *sickness* which thou canst not heal. There is no fall, however great, for which thou hast not compassion and an instinctive, irresistible desire to repair.

Riches of the soul. The riches of the soul are virtues. To other creatures virtues are given *separately;* to Mary they were given as a whole. Virtues form her diadem, her vesture, her whole being.

Count, says a saint, the stars, count the drops of dew which appear each morning, multiply them again and then again, and yet you will say the virtues of Mary's soul are still more numerous.

Mary! O treasure of God! O riches of God! O splendor of God! Why am I not dazzled by thy magnificence? Human grandeur awes and withholds us; how is it that I feel myself drawn to thee, reassured by thee, and that near thee I am tranquil, happy, and simply and completely at my ease? Ah, it is because of thy goodness, O Mary!

THE LORD IS WITH THEE.

Behold the secret of that ever new, ever irresistible attraction which wins the just as well as sinners.

The *good God* is with thee, the good God is visible through thy glance, through thy hands, through thy heart, and it is He who attracts us.

God within thee means grace.
God within thee means mercy.
God within thee means peace.

Ah, Mary, since thou art so kind, since thou art so rich, thou who possessest God, give me, give me this dear Jesus!

Like thee I receive Him in Holy Communion; may I like thee, O Mary, bear Him everywhere with me!

May I make His presence felt about me, that those with whom my life is united may say to me in the words of the Angel: *The Lord is with thee!*

BLESSED ART THOU AMONG WOMEN.

More than all creatures art thou praised, exalted, glorified by all who can comprehend and love thee!

Blessed in heaven by the angels and the saints.

Blessed by God the Father, who contemplates in thee His holiest, most beautiful, most loving creature, one in whom He has, so to speak, exhausted His power.

Blessed by the Holy Spirit, who has

made thee His temple in which He abides, and which He unceasingly fills with splendor, purity, peace.

Blessed by the Son of God, who is ever thy *Jesus*, Jesus, the loving, submissive child who still calls thee *mother;* Jesus, whose infant heart bounds each time He hears us say to thee, *Hail Mary!*

Upon earth also art thou *blessed*, and this earthly benediction is no less sweet to thy heart.

It unceasingly ascends from the hearts of those whom thou hast assisted, comforted, and strengthened.

The poor, the afflicted, the unfortunate *bless* thee; the mother *blesses* thee; the child *blesses* thee; the spouses of God *bless* thee; His priests *bless* thee.

Oh, let me join my voice to the voice of all creatures, to the voice particularly of Jesus, in the Eucharist, to praise, to love thee with Him!

AND BLESSED IS THE FRUIT OF THY WOMB, JESUS.

It is to the tabernacle where Thou art truly present, O Jesus, Son of Mary, that I now turn my gaze and bear my grateful heart!

Yes, be *blessed* for having given us Mary for our mother, our guardian, our refuge, our model!

Be blessed for having made her so great, so exalted, and particularly so compassionate!

For it is to *Thee*, O Jesus, that we must turn to find the ever fruitful source of all grace; it is in *Thee* that we must rest as the beginning and the end of all greatness and all sanctity; it is Thee whom we must thank as the one only being who possesseth all things by nature, who giveth all things in goodness; it is Thee whom Mary teaches us to exalt and glorify, because all that she has she possesses only through Thee!

II.

Confidence and Prayer.

HOLY MARY, MOTHER OF GOD.

Mother of God! Behold thy supreme title, the foundation of thy glory, the end for which God created thee immaculate, and filled thee with all those virtues, all those graces, all those gifts which made thee the strongest, the tenderest, the most loving, the most devoted of mothers.

Mother of God! Behold the foundation of the homage which since the birth of thy divine Son all hearts which know and love Jesus offer thee with joy, respect, and veneration,—the foundation particularly of that confidence which nothing, nothing throughout all ages shall ever diminish!

Wert thou not the *Mother of God*, I could love thee for thy virtues, for thy tender heart; but I should not be as I am now at thy feet waiting, confident that I shall not be repelled, that I shall not be disappointed, waiting thy powerful aid in the *salvation of my soul.*

Wert thou not *Mother of God,* God would love thee for thy *purity,* would appreciate and reward thy *sanctity;* but thou wouldst not of *necessity,* so to speak, be heard each time thou didst ask a grace of that Son who was so submissive to thee upon earth.

Mother of God! This title alone justifies, sanctions, consecrates all the inventions of gratitude, all the transports of the soul, all the inspirations of tender love meant to honor, bless, and glorify upon earth her whom God Himself has honored with an infinite dignity.

PRAY FOR US SINNERS.

Consoling words! At this very moment that I am speaking to Mary, the good God permits Mary to hear me.

If Mary hears me I am sure she will

heed me; if thou hearest me, Mary, wilt thou not obtain what I ask?

If formerly, passing along the way, thou heardst the voice of a suppliant calling to thee, thou wouldst not have passed without stopping to listen to him.

If this poor suppliant said to thee, *I am hungry*, thou wouldst not have passed without giving him an alms.

If he showed thee a wound, thou wouldst not have passed without comforting him.

Wilt thou be less kind in heaven?

Since my voice reaches thee, hear me, O my mother! *I am hungry*, great is my soul's hunger! I hunger for purity, I hunger for devotedness, I hunger for piety! *Pray for me.*

She is hungry, that soul who is not here near thee, that soul whom I love and who knows thee not; she is hungry, that soul who knew thee and has forgotten thee. Oh, give them some crumbs of that grace, that light, that salutary remorse which God has given thee to bring back souls!

Mary! Pray for us sinners.

NOW.

Yes, *now;* my need is urgent, my petition presses. Hear me, O Mary!

Seest thou not the demon of sensuality that awaits me at the door of that chapel where I am wont to pray?

Seest thou not those evil spirits who surround me, and who, if I do not vigilantly guard my soul with piety and labor, will gradually penetrate it with thoughts of *vanity*, of *antipathy*, of *vengeance*, of *disgust for my duty*, of *weariness in prayer*, of *distrust of my superiors?*

Seest thou not that the soul of which I just spoke to you is on the point of yielding to temptation?

Mary, pray for her, pray for me, pray *now!*

⁎
⁎

AND AT THE HOUR OF OUR DEATH.

As I utter these words, many souls surprised by death are entering their eternity, and at the end of the day more than *eighty thousand* shall have appeared before God. Ah, if they have invoked thee, O Mary, what rejoicing there will be in heaven! The supreme moment must come for me, yes, for *me!* Shall it be ten years hence? Shall it be to-morrow? Shall it be to-night?

O Mary, Mary, whom I have so often invoked, be at my couch in this hour; take the place my mother would fill were she still with me! Perhaps my speechless lips can no longer pronounce thy name, but my heart will utter it with every pulsation.

Wilt thou not be with me, Mother of Jesus and my mother? I *invoke* thee now for the hour *of my death.* And in my appeal I rest calm and tranquil. Yes, though expiring alone, far from all succor, with no loving hand to close my eyes, I shall die content, for thou wilt be present, O Mary, faithful to the meeting which I now appoint with thee, thou wilt be with me I believe, I hope, I am confident.

AMEN.

XLIV.

HOW GOD BRINGS BACK SOULS.

Do you know how the rule of St. Francis of Assissi proceeds to make a man a saint?

It takes a man and takes from him everything he has, and putting a bag on his back and a cord around his neck, tells him, *Go now; you shall be so unhappy on earth that you will be obliged to go to heaven.*

It is thus that God is sometimes obliged to treat certain souls, to whom, nevertheless, he has given every facility for walking in the path to heaven.

Poor souls, to whom the earth was very bright, too bright for their souls, and who, in answer to God's appeals, ever replied, *Later, my God*, and who would have ended by gradually wasting all the love God had given them, and which God asked of them.

To bring back these souls God gradually takes from them *joys of heart*. They lose the love which formerly surrounded them, and they feel that it is through their own fault. They have been sustained, applauded, encouraged, and they find themselves neglected, distrusted, despised, and for no apparent reason.

God allows them to fall into imprudences, and these imprudences, committed innocently and exaggerated through malice, jealousy, or even imprudent zeal, cause them to be severely condemned, and gradually friends fall off, until she who was formerly so beloved suddenly finds herself deserted and knows not where to turn for sympathy. Oh, who can tell the pain, the suffering, the anguish of these souls unfaithful to God's call?

God also takes from her *joys of mind*. Her path is bright and clear before her, she goes through life careless and happy, when suddenly clouds obscure her path, all is dark, trouble invades her soul, she becomes the victim of doubt and scruples, she believes herself a burden to those about her, she imagines that those in whom she was wont to trust repel her, and fearing to ask counsel, and not daring to act without guidance, she finds herself alone in a pathless, dark, and sunless desert. Oh, again who shall say the fear, the terror, which overwhelm these poor souls unfaithful to God's call?

Then in one of those hours bordering on despair the soul whom God has thus gradually impoverished, and who is on the point of yielding to murmurs, hears a voice which penetrates her more deeply than the fire penetrates the wood which it consumes—God's voice, which the soul understands, and, overcome by hunger and thirst, that hunger of soul and thirst of heart a thousand times more terrible than any other, she says, *I will rise and go to my Father!*

And she goes to her Father, to her God who awaits her, who clasps her in His arms, and for all reproach murmurs, *Why hast thou tarried, my child?* My God! My God! How great are Thy love and tenderness! And how shall eternity suffice to thank Thee!

***

My God, my Father! let me be so

unhappy, so neglected, so little loved on earth that, impelled by my imperious thirst for happiness, for love, I may give myself completely to Thee!

XLV.

A friend meeting the Abbé Pereyve, who had just been preaching, and finding him bathed in perspiration, said:

But you are wearing yourself out, my friend!

Ah, replied the Abbé, *what is a priest good for who does not wear himself out?*

Christian soul, remember these words. Make them thine. Behold thy duty: To give, to spend, to wear thyself out for God and souls. The souls who spare themselves shall not enter heaven.

XLVI.

THAT WHICH COULD MAKE ME UNHAPPY.

It was evening after one of those family gatherings which unlike worldly reunions leave no trouble in the soul, but rather a perfume of peace and sweetness, like the breath of spring upon the flowers.

Evening had come, and silence reigned in the sumptuous house but an hour before filled with happy faces and joyous laughter; it was one of those feasts which gently refresh the soul, and from which the guardian angel of the family has no need to turn and hide his face; everything about it breathed candor, frankness, and purity.

The young girl for whom the feast was given, after embracing and thanking her parents, kneels before her crucifix, and raising her eyes to the beloved image exclaims in the fulness of her heart, *My God, how good Thou art to me, how happy Thou dost make me!*

Then suddenly across her joy like a cloud over the blue sky comes the thought, *What would make me unhappy?*

And after a moment's silence the

young girl rises, and seating herself at her work table writes the following pages:

What would rob me of this sweet and peaceful happiness which fills my whole being? *What would make me unhappy?*

Would the *loss of my fortune?* Ah, no, no! One can be happy without wealth I know; and but for the inability to do good it seems to me I could readily accept poverty. I do not know why, but when I have heard those about me, particularly lately, say, *She is rich*, it inspires me with a sort of disgust. Can it be that I am loved and esteemed for my wealth? Oh, in that case I would not have it!

What would make me unhappy?

Would *less cleverness?* After all one can be happy without being very clever. Does not the greater part of my ill-humor, my humiliations, my estrangements, my interrupted friendships come from the abuse or at least the parade of my cleverness? With more heart and less cleverness should I not have been more kind and more forbearing? Would I not have pardoned more readily? Would I have been so quick to see the mistake which led me a few days since to humble and wound a friend to tears? No, doubtless I would not be devoid of cleverness, but I should fear to be too clever.

WHAT WOULD MAKE ME UNHAPPY?

Would—I hesitate a little to write it—would the loss of *my exterior beauty*? If I were to become ugly or only *less attractive*, would I be unhappy? This question gives me a slight tremor which I will not try to explain, but after all—no, beauty does not make one *happy*, for it does not of itself make one *good*. Beauty may attract hearts, but it does not retain them; then beauty fades. Do I not love my good and pious H—— in spite of her plainness? Is she not always cheerful and pleasant? Do I not feel in her presence that soothing rest and calm and peace which her interior beauty, that is her goodness, seems to communicate to me? Ah, yes, beauty of countenance may leave me, provided that penetrating interiorly it be changed into virtue!

WHAT THEN WOULD MAKE ME UNHAPPY?

Would it be *to lose the affection of those who love me?* O my God, my God, if my loved ones were to turn from me, if there were created a desert about my heart, if I saw that, becoming indifferent to me, they distrusted me, cruelly misjudged me, neglected me, fled from me, accorded me only their pity!

No, no, this is not possible while thou livest, O my mother, while thou livest, O companion of my first communion, O sister, not given by God, but whom I choose!

Yet, my father, my mother gone, all the others could tire of loving me, and then?

Then Thou wouldst remain to me, my God! for thou lovest always! Thou canst not but love! And with *Thee for my friend* I should not be unhappy!

WHAT THEN WOULD MAKE ME UNHAPPY?

Ah, I see it, I know it, and I hope, my God, that I may never, never experience it.

A *remorseful pang* in the depth of my soul is sufficient. My God, my God, spare me *remorse*, and consequently the *fault* which gives rise to it!

XLVII.

THE SONG OF THE CONSCIENCE.

Go on thy way calmly and cheerfully, brave and generous child, whose cheeks have lost the freshness of youth, from long vigils spent in labor for thy sick mother, and thy little brothers, incapable of earning bread, go on thy way, and lower not thy eyes before these companions who laugh at thy pallid brow and thy shoulders bent with labor!

Go calmly and proudly on thy way, pure young girl, hearing about thee the partially smothered laughter excited by thy poor and modest dress, and the poignant gibes of those voices, which formerly cried to thee *Come with us; there is gold and pleasure to be had*, and which thou didst repel, saying, *My mother forbids it*.

Go on thy way with head erect,

magnanimous heart assailed by the venom of calumny, and who hast found thyself deserted by all, and perhaps thy livelihood taken from thee, because, faithful to thy God, faithful to the promises of thy first communion, thou hast continued an honest, industrious girl, never turned from thy duty by human respect, nor weakened by perfidious promises.

* *
*

And let not thy peace be disturbed, but remain calm and strong, thou who, by one of those mysterious dispensations the secret of which is God's, knowest not how *to be amiable* in thy family, though thy heart overflows with affection, knowest not how to make thy *services available* though thy labor is greater than that of all, and who doth remain despised, rejected, regarded as useless, continue thy daily devotedness in isolation and neglect, pray, love, labor in silence, let others profit by thy labor, and reap the renown which is thine.

I am with you, to strengthen you, to encourage you, to sustain you, to love you—hidden martyrs to duty, to duty performed in obscurity, under the eyes of God alone; I, your conscience, am with you; I, who will be more loving in proportion as the world is more disdainful; I, who see all thy suffering, all thy prodigal devotion and self-denial—I, whom nothing can deceive, because *I am the light of God.*

I am with you, *your conscience*, incorruptible witness and judge; I am with you, abiding in the depth of your soul, having received, for tried and faithful souls like yours mysterious balm, ineffable sweetness, powerful and heavenly succor.

With me thou art never alone, with me thou art never defenceless, to hear from my lips the simple words, *I am content with thee* is to count as naught neglect, contempt, the bitterest pangs.

Happiness on earth is delusive and passes like a shadow; friendship weakens, wearies, leaves us; hope fades and deceives us. But I survive happiness, friendship, hope; I live always, my smile never fades.

Courage then, tried but ever faithful soul; courage, crushed but ever devoted heart. *I love thee, I love thee, and I am content with thee.* With me for friend one may be poor, yet know happiness, one may be despised, yet feel one's dignity, one may want for everything, one may live unknown and neglected, one may be unable to restrain one's tears, yet hear in the depth of his soul, like an echo from heaven, the words, *I am content with thee!*

Then cease to hang thy head; that

becomes only the guilty, and thou art not guilty, poor despised one, thou art only afflicted; and suffering is an aureole on thy brow, in the eyes of the angels.

*_**

'Envy not the wealth of this companion, the elevated rank of that one, the rich toilet of that former friend, the affection which seems to thee to be lavished upon another. Thou seest them only when they are cradled in *false dreams.* Alone in that solitude, that terrible solitude which comes sooner or later when riches, position, friendly smiles have disappeared — ah, what would they not give to hear my voice, my loved voice murmuring to them the words I whisper to thee, poor neglected one, *I am content with thee!*

Courage then! and when the dream of *this present* life shall be forever ended, I will lead thee to that life which shall never end; and both of us intimately united, thou the dove and I thy wings, shall fly to our repose in the bosom of God, where is rest and light and love.

XLVIII.

LITANY OF GOODNESS AND DEVOTION.

O Jesus! living in the Holy Eucharist, but living silent and inactive, void of that material life which falls under the senses, and consequently unable to make men *feel* Thy goodness and mercy as in the days of Thy mortal life; Jesus, who nevertheless desirest that men *feel* Thy love; I come to offer myself to Thee, that, communicating Thyself to me, dwelling within me, Thou mayest use all the members of my body, all the faculties of my soul, to do for those whom Thou lovest what Thou wert wont to do for them on earth when Thou wast visibly present with them.

O Jesus! abandoned by all in the Garden of Olives, with no one to comfort, to strengthen, to encourage Thee; Jesus, who knowest that at this hour there are souls who, like Thee, have no longer any support, strength, or consolation on earth; send them an angel to pour into their souls a little joy, a little peace! Oh, that I might fill that angelic mission! What must I suffer to that end, O Jesus? If there be needed an interior trial or exterior sorrow to make me for a few moments the consoling angel of a desolate soul, Oh, whatever the bitterness of that trial, whatever the duration of that sorrow, I ask it of Thee, O Jesus!

O Jesus, who seekest *lips* to tell souls of the love Thou bearest them; lips to remind the poor and the outcast that they are not abandoned, the *guilty*, that they are not despised, the *timid*, that they are protected; Jesus, take my *lips*, and without my knowledge, if it is to be feared that vanity may spoil what comes but from Thee, give me to speak or write words of strength, of love, of kindness, of pardon. Grant that I may consider a day lost in which I shall not have spoken of Thy goodness, in which I shall not have raised up or fortified a soul, in which I shall not have caused Thy name to be uttered with love at least by a little child!

O Jesus, *so patient* with those who tried Thee by their importunity, and who wearied Thee by their ignorance and their slowness in comprehending Thy words; Jesus, so kind in repeating the same lessons, in waiting the hour of grace rather than humiliate those who seemed to be indifferent to Thy doctrine; Jesus, make me *patient* to *listen*, patient to *instruct*, patient to begin over again the same lessons three, four, ten times. Make me *strong* to preserve in my countenance a kind expression, even when the importunity of a visitor weighs heavily upon me; and if the weakness of my temperament overcome my will, and I allow my weariness and fatigue to be visible, O Jesus, give me to quickly repair, by loving words, the pain I may have caused!

O Jesus, who with infinite delicacy didst wait on the roadside the opportunity to do good, who didst simply ask a material service to approach more easily the soul of the Samaritan woman whom Thou didst seek to save; Jesus give me to *divine* the sorrow which timidity sometimes, more frequently fear, or even an exaggerated delicacy conceals in the depth of the soul; give me that simple, courageous, but discreet tact which insinuates itself without wounding, which asks without irritating, and which without humiliating pours oil and wine into the wound it has discovered.

O Jesus, who seekest a faithful dispenser of Thy *material treasures* and of those exterior joys, the reflection of the ineffable joys of heaven, give me much, that I may bestow much; take *my hands* and make them the dispensers of Thy alms; take them that like Thine, when Thou didst wash the feet of Thy Disciples, they *may be at the service of all, laboring for all, coming to the assistance of all.* Grant that I may never forget that like Thee I am on earth *to serve, not to be served.* Take my lips, also, that they may give to hearts *joyous words* and *cheering smiles.* O Jesus, may I be like the fountain on the wayside where all may be refreshed, may I be like the tree by the roadside which is the property of no one, and belongs to all, which offers to the passing traveller the shade of its branches laden with the fruit God has lent it for others.

*_**

O Jesus, who passionately lovest souls, and who never permittest Thyself, spite of pleasing or repellant exteriors, docile or unquiet minds, gentle or irascible tempers, to forget that these souls, even the coarsest, are God's beloved children; grant me in my relations with those about me to see but their souls, to love but their souls, to help them but with a view to their souls, these souls, O Jesus, for whom Thou didst die, who in truth may with me call Thee *Father*, and with whom near Thee in the intimacy of Thy heart I am to live for a happy eternity.

END.

Volumes 1 to 8 now ready.

THE CENTENARY EDITION.

ASCETICAL WORKS OF ST. ALPHONSUS
18 vols., Price, per vol., net, $1.25.

Each book complete in itself,—any volume sold separately.

Vol. I. PREPARATION FOR DEATH; or, Considerations on the Eternal Truths. Maxims of Eternity—Rule of Life.

Vol. II. WAY OF SALVATION AND OF PERFECTION: Meditations. Pious Reflections. Spiritual Treatises.

Vol. III. GREAT MEANS OF SALVATION AND OF PERFECTION: Prayer. Mental Prayer. The Exercises of a Retreat. Choice of a State of Life, and the Vocation to the Religious State and to the Priesthood.

Vol. IV., V., VI. THE MYSTERIES OF THE FAITH: 1. Incarnation, Birth and Infancy of Jesus Christ. 2. The Redemption, Passion and Death of Jesus Christ. 3. The Holy Eucharist, Sacrifice, and Sacred Heart of Jesus Christ. Practice of Love of Jesus Christ. Novena to the Holy Ghost.

Vol. VII., VIII. GLORIES OF MARY: 1. Explanation of the *Salve Regina*, or Hail, Holy Queen. Discourses on the Feasts of Mary. 2. Her Dolors. Her Virtues. Practices. Examples. Answers to Critics—Devotion to the Holy Angels. Devotion to St. Joseph. Novena to St. Teresa. Novena for the Repose of the Souls in Purgatory.

Vol. IX. VICTORIES OF THE MARTYRS; or, The Lives of the Most Celebrated Martyrs of the Church.

Vol. X., XI. THE TRUE SPOUSE OF JESUS CHRIST: 1. The first sixteen Chapters. 2. The last eight Chapters. Appendix and various small Works. Spiritual Letters.

Vol. XII. CONGREGATION OF THE MOST HOLY REDEEMER: Rule. Instructions about the Religious State. Letters and Circulars. Lives of two Fathers and of a Lay-brother.

Vol. XIII. DIGNITY AND DUTIES OF THE PRIEST: A Collection of Material for Ecclesiastical Retreats. Rule of Life and Spiritual Rules.

Vol. XIV. THE HOLY MASS: Sacrifice of Jesus Christ. Ceremonies of the Mass. Preparation and Thanksgiving. The Mass and the Office that are hurriedly said.

Vol. XV. THE DIVINE OFFICE: Translation of the Psalms and Hymns.

Vol. XVI. PREACHING: The Exercises of the Missions. Various Counsels. Instructions on the Commandments and Sacraments.

Vol. XVII. SERMONS FOR THE SUNDAYS.

Vol. XVIII. VARIOUS SMALL WORKS: Discourses on Calamities. Reflections useful for Bishops. Seminaries. Ordinances. Letters. General Alphabetical Index.

BENZIGER BROTHERS, New York, Cincinnati, and Chicago.

The Centenary Edition.

THE COMPLETE WORKS OF
St. Alphonsus de Liguori.

Translated from the Italian.
Edited by Rev. EUGENE GRIMM, C.SS.R.

18 Vols., Price per Vol., net, $1.25.

Each book is complete in itself, any volume will be sold separately.

Subscriptions solicited for the Complete Works.

In commemoration of the One Hundredth Anniversary of the death of their founder which occurs in the year 1887, the Redemptorist Fathers have undertaken the publication of a new and the only complete uniform edition in English of the ASCETICAL AND DOGMATICAL WORKS OF SAINT ALPHONSUS. It will contain many explanatory notes which will enable the reader to understand more fully the writings of the holy Doctor. It was usual with the saintly author to insert in his works **Latin Scripture texts and Latin quotations** from the Fathers. This method is also followed in this new English edition. The Latin texts will, however, be given as foot-notes. The sacred poetry composed by the Saint will be found interspersed through the different volumes of the ascetical works. Besides the table of contents, each volume will contain an alphabetical index.

PREPARATION FOR DEATH;
OR,
Considerations on the Eternal Truths,
USEFUL FOR ALL AS MEDITATIONS AND
SERVICEABLE TO PRIESTS FOR SERMONS.
(Maxims of Eternity—Rule of Life.)

THE WAY OF SALVATION
AND
OF PERFECTION.
Meditations—Pious Reflections—Spiritual Treatises.

BENZIGER BROTHERS, New York, Cincinnati, and Chicago.

35th Thousand.—Reduced from $3.50 to $2.00.

"Let the adornments of home be chaste and holy pictures and, still more, **sound and profitable books.**"
Pastoral Letter of the Third Plenary Council of Baltimore.

PICTORIAL
Lives of the Saints.

With Reflections for Every Day in the Year.

Compiled from "Butler's Lives" and other Approved Sources. To which are added **Lives of the American Saints** recently placed on the Calendar for the United States by Special Petition of the Third Plenary Council of Baltimore. And also **Lives of the Saints Canonized in 1881** by His Holiness Pope Leo XIII.

EDITED BY JOHN GILMARY SHEA, LL.D.

Large 8vo. 538 pages, rich ink and gold side. With nearly 400 Illustrations.

Reduced Price, - - - - **$2.00**

This, **the cheapest and most attractive work published,** has been greatly admired by

OUR HOLY FATHER, POPE LEO XIII.,

who sent his special blessing to the publishers.

It has also received the warm approbation of the Archbishops and Bishops in every section of the country, and cannot be too highly recommended to Christian families as the

Best Reading for the Home Circle.

It offers in a compendious form the lives of many servants of God, forming, as it were, **a book of daily meditations,** and is embellished with nearly

FOUR HUNDRED ILLUSTRATIONS,

including a beautiful frontispiece of the Holy Family, a full-page picture of St. Patrick, the glorious Apostle of Ireland, made expressly for this work from a fine steel engraving, and two other full-page engravings making **an illustration for almost every life given.**

BENZIGER BROTHERS, New York, Cincinnati, and Chicago.

60th Thousand.

Catholic Belief:

Or A Short and Simple Exposition of Catholic Doctrine. By the Very Rev. JOSEPH FAA DI BRUNO, D.D. American Edition edited by Rev. LOUIS A. LAMBERT, author of "Notes on Ingersoll," etc. With the Imprimatur of Their Eminences the late Cardinal, Archbishop of New York, and the Cardinal, Archbishop of Westminster, and an Introduction by the Right Rev. S. V. RYAN, Bishop of Buffalo.

16mo, flexible cloth, 40 cents.
10 copies, $2.65.—50 copies, $12.00,—100 copies, $20.00.
Extra cloth, red edges, 75 cents.

An admirable book of instruction on Christian Doctrine for both Catholics and Protestants. Short, clear, simple, and concise it meets the needs of a numerous class of non-Catholics, who yearning after Truth, unsettled in their convictions, sincere in their inquiries, and curious to know just what Catholics do believe, have neither leisure nor inclination to pore over large volumes or study elaborate dogmatical treatises. The author evinces rare ability and tact in setting forth Catholic principles in a few words, with winning simplicity and yet scholastic accuracy, but entire freedom from anything which might give offence to any one, without, however, compromising or disguising, the truth. The book is just the one to put in the hands of a Protestant friend, confident that Catholic faith will more readily reach the soul and bring conviction to the understanding, when Catholic charity has won the heart and favorably predisposed the will.

———o———

Catholic Home Almanac.

A Charming Annual for Catholics.

Single copies, 25 cents; per dozen, $2.00.

Pure, wholesome reading for the Home Circle, of interest to young and old.

A Choice Collection of Prose and Verse, embracing Short Stories — humorous and pathetic — Poems, Historical and Biographical Sketches, Anecdotes, Statistics, Astronomical Calculations, etc., with numerous beautiful illustrations and the Calendars for the months printed in black and red, making it just the book for winter evenings.

BENZIGER BROTHERS, New York, Cincinnati, and Chicago.

The Glories of Divine Grace.

A free rendering of the original treatise of P. EUSEBIUS NIEREMBERG, S.J.

By Dr. M. JOS. SCHEEBEN.

Translated from the fourth revised German edition, by a **BENEDICTINE MONK** of St. Meinrad's Abbey, Ind., with the consent of the Author and the permission of the Superior.

12mo, cloth, - - $1.50

The book treats of the nature of grace; of the sublime and incomprehensible union with God, to which grace leads us; of the effects and fruits of grace; of some other effects and prerogatives of divine grace; and of the acquisition, exercise, increase and preservation of grace. **It is a mine of the richest material for sermons, catechism and the confessional,** and will also prove highly valuable to both religious and pious people in the world.

Little Compliments of the Season.

Simple Verses for Name-days, Birthdays, Christmas, New-Year, and other festive and social occasions. With numerous and appropriate illustrations.

By ELEANOR C. DONNELLY.

16mo, cloth, ink and gold, $1.00

Life of St. Germaine Cousin.

The Shepherd Maiden of Pibrac.

Translated from the French by a **SISTER OF MERCY**.

With a Frontispiece, 16mo, cloth, 50 cents.

Glistening Grains from "Golden Sands."

A series of six leaflets, comprising: A Thought for the New Year—Litany of Goodness and Devotion—To make Friends—Our Mother Mary—Sanctification—The Sacred Heart.

Paper, gilt edges, 5 cents each; Per 100, $3.00

BENZIGER BROTHERS, New York, Cincinnati, and Chicago.

MEDITATIONS ON THE
Sufferings of Jesus Christ.

Translated from the Italian of
Rev. FRANCIS da PERINALDO, O.S.F.,
By a Member of the same Order.
12mo, Cloth, $1.25.

This work, the original of which has run through four editions in a short time, is, according to an able critic, "good in thought, sentiment, and expression: the thought being just, solid, and conformable to Catholic teaching; the sentiment tender and devotional; the expression or language generally plain and unpretending, but, when occasion demands, rising to a dignity and pathos suited to the persons and subjects described."

St. Joseph, the Advocate of Hopeless Cases.

Translated from the French of
Rev. Father HUGUET, Marist.
32mo, Cloth, $1.00.

The pious and learned author of this work offers it in the hope that the touching traits of the goodness and power of St. Joseph, herein set forth, may inspire all who read with unlimited confidence in the intercession of this blessed Patriarch, who enjoyed the happiness of passing thirty years in the intimate society of the Mother of Divine Mercy and of the Son of God come down from Heaven to redeem us.

A Thought from St. Ignatius
FOR EVERY DAY OF THE YEAR.

Translated from the French by Miss Margaret A. Colton.
With a Steel-plate Frontispiece.
32mo, Cloth, - - - - 50 Cts.

BENZIGER BROTHERS, New York, Cincinnati, and Chicago.

Abandonment;
OR,
ABSOLUTE SURRENDER OF SELF
TO
DIVINE PROVIDENCE.

By Rev. J. P. CAUSSADE, S.J.

Edited and Revised by Rev. H. Ramière, S.J.

Translated from the French by Miss ELLA McMAHON.

32mo, Cloth, - - - 50 Cts.

Hand-book for Altar Societies
AND GUIDE FOR SACRISTANS,
And Others Having Charge of the Altar and Sanctuary.

By a Member of an Altar Society.

Published with the Imprimatur of the Right Rev. Francis McNeirny, D.D., Bishop of Albany.

16mo, cloth, red edges, - - net, 75 cents.

There are many pious hearts and willing hands in every congregation, ready to take charge of the Altar and Sanctuary, and prepare them for the various services and solemnities of religion. All they need is proper direction. Comparatively few congregations in this country are able to have religious communities to superintend the requirements of the Altar and Sanctuary, and as our Altar Societies are composed of ladies, willing, but inexperienced in this important work, it occurred to the author that a guide-book of practical suggestions and directions would be of great service in every parish. The book not only gives all necessary instruction concerning the preparations enjoined by the Rubrics for each and every service, but also treats of decorations (both within and without the Sanctuary) appropriate to the various festivals of the year, together with the information requisite for the proper carrying out of the Church Ceremonial.

BENZIGER BROTHERS, New York, Cincinnati, and Chicago.

GREETINGS
TO THE
CHRIST-CHILD.

A Collection of Christmas Poems for the Young.

EMBELLISHED WITH 89 ILLUSTRATIONS, TAILPIECES, ETC., ETC.

Square 16mo, on fine, super-calendered, tinted paper, full gilt back. and elegant side stamp in gold, 50c.

BENZIGER BROTHERS, New York, Cincinnati, and Chicago.

Words of the Saints.

A THOUGHT FROM ST. FRANCIS OF ASSISI, and his Saints, for Every Day of the Year. Translated from the French by Miss MARGARET A. COLTON. With a steel-plate Frontispiece, 32mo, cloth, ... 50 cents.

The voice of the Supreme Pontiff has so stirred the devotion of the faithful for the Seraph of Assisi and his "Army of Saints" that the publishers are encouraged to issue this little book in the hope that it will prove opportune and acceptable.

A THOUGHT FROM ST. ALPHONSUS, For Every Day of the Year. Translated from the French by ANNA T. SADLIER. With a steel-plate Frontispiece. 32mo, cloth, ... 50 cents.

As a memorial of the great Saint's Centennial, this little book ought to be heartily welcomed by the faithful.

THOUGHTS FROM DOMINICAN SAINTS, For Every Day in the Year. Translated from the French by a Sister of Mercy. With a steel-plate Frontispiece. 32mo, cloth...................... ..... 50 cents.

MAXIMS AND COUNSELS OF ST. FRANCIS DE SALES, for Every Day of the Year. Translated from the French by Miss ELLA McMAHON. With a steel-plate Frontispiece. 32mo, cloth, 50 cents.

This collection is like the inner life of the Saint unconsciously written by himself. *These counsels have been carefully gleaned from the complete collection of the Holy Doctor of the Church.*

A THOUGHT OF ST. TERESA'S, For Every Day in the Year. Translated from the French by Miss ELLA McMAHON. With a steel-plate Frontispiece. 32mo, extra cloth,.............. 50 cents.

This little book contains the most precious thoughts of one of the greatest mystic writers of the Church. Short and to the point, these thoughts, it is hop d, may soon become familiar to the lips of American Catholics.

BENZIGER BROTHERS, New York, Cincinnati, and Chicago.

Month of the Dead;

OR,

PROMPT AND EASY DELIVERANCE OF THE SOULS IN PURGATORY.

Translated from the French of
THE ABBÉ CLOQUET,
Honorary Canon, Apostolic Missionary and Late Vicar-General,

BY A SISTER OF MERCY.

Approved by the Sacred Congregation and by His Lordship, the Archbishop of Bourges, and His Grace, the Archbishop of New York.

With a steel-plate Frontispiece. 32mo, cloth, 75 cents.

This little book is particularly **rich in Indulgenced Prayers applicable to the Suffering Souls in Purgatory,** one entire part being devoted to them. They can be relied on as correct, since they have not only been compared with the RACCOLTA but they also bear the **special approbation of the Sacred Congregation of Indulgences.**

BENZIGER BROTHERS, New York, Cincinnati, and Chicago.

New Year Greetings.

By St. Francis de Sales. Translated from the French by Miss Margaret A. Colton.

32mo, maroquette, full gilt side, 15 cts.; per 100, $10.00.

This little book breathing words of love and tenderness, of peace and happiness for the New Year, so characteristic of the gentle Doctor of the Church, is eminently suited not only for a New Year's Gift, but will provide **spiritual reading for the whole year.**

Meditations on the Passion of Our Lord.

Together with a Manual of the Black Scapular of the Passion; and Daily Prayers. Translated from the Italian by a Passionist Father. With Frontispiece and 14 full-page Illustrations of the Way of the Cross.

32mo, cloth, red edges, 40 cents.

The aim of this little book is to assist in meditating on the Passion of Christ, and is intended especially for those who cannot procure or would, perhaps, shrink from reading works in which the inexhaustible subject of the Passion is treated more learnedly and at greater length. It contains short and simple meditations that will suggest matter for pious reflection, and may move to sentiments of compassion and love for our suffering Redeemer.

Memorial of a Christian Life.

Containing all that a Soul newly converted to God ought to do, that it may attain the perfection to which it should aspire. From the Spanish of the Ven. Lewis de Granada. With a Preface by a Dominican Father of New York. 16mo, cloth, ...**60 cents.**

The author of this book was a most profound and practical master of spiritual life. Pope Gregory XIII., during whose pontificate he composed many of his works, often testified that this writer had done more in the cause of the Church than if he had raised the dead to life and had given sight to the blind. St. Charles Borromeo was equally lavish of praise; and St. Francis de Sales constantly recommended these books to all under his spiritual guidance.

BENZIGER BROTHERS, New York, Cincinnati, and Chicago.

Our Birthday Bouquet,

Culled from the Shrines of the Saints and the Gardens of the Poets.

By E. C. DONNELLY.

16mo, cloth, $1.00; full gilt, $1.25.

A Miniature Lives of the Saints, containing a short "Life" for every day of the year, followed by an appropriate verse from some standard Poet, and concluding with a devotional practice for the day. It fully sustains the high name of its gifted author in the domain of spiritual literature.

MAXIMS AND COUNSELS
OF
St. Francis de Sales

For Every Day of the Year.

Translated from the French by Miss ELLA McMAHON.

32mo, cloth, 50 cents.

This collection is like the inner life of the Saint unconsciously written by himself. He first practised, and then taught. One is gentle from motives of virtue, only when he possesses moral strength; in these lines we find the secret of that strength which made St. Francis de Sales the gentlest of men. He admirably inculcates the method of sanctity which he perfectly possessed, a sanctity which seems so easy to realize that we feel a desire to reproduce it. It is the flower which the Saint causes to bloom in your soul, and which will soon bear fruit if you are faithful. These counsels have been carefully gleaned from the complete collection of the Holy Doctor of the Church.

BENZIGER BROTHERS, New York, Cincinnati and Chicago.

A BOOK FOR THE FAMILY!

GOFFINE'S
DEVOUT INSTRUCTIONS
ON THE EPISTLES AND GOSPELS.

For the Sundays and Holidays; with Explanations of Christian Faith and Duty and of Church Ceremonies. By the Rev. LEONARD GOFFINE. Translated by the Rev. THEO. NOETHEN.
With 8 Full-page Illustrations.

Crown 8vo. Cloth, ink and gold side. $1.50.
        "   "   "   "   gilt edges,   2.00.

As a work of spiritual reading and instruction GOFFINE'S DEVOUT INSTRUCTIONS stands in the foremost rank. In it the faithful will find explained in a plain, simple manner the doctrines of the Church, her sacraments and ceremonies, as set forth in the Epistles and Gospels of the Sundays and holy days. The Catholic Church has at all times joined instruction with the offering of the Holy Sacrifice. But as the words of the speaker pass away and are forgotten, it is proper that preaching and spiritual reading should support each other. By this means instruction is more deeply impressed on the heart, and much that we might lose by neglect may thus be preserved. For these reasons, the reading of spiritual books is recommended as a means of properly keeping Sundays and holy days.

By the help of this book, those who are prevented by just cause from assisting at Mass may be enabled to arrange their family devotions. In Europe, the original of GOFFINE'S INSTRUCTIONS is extensively used for this purpose, and it is not only recommended and circulated there by the Bishops and priests, but some of the most learned and distinguished German divines have from time to time edited it.

The translator of the present Edition, which is undoubtedly **the best English version**, has not restricted himself to the text of any one Edition, but has made use of several of those that are most esteemed.

BENZIGER BROTHERS, New York, Cincinnati, and Chicago.

NEW, ENLARGED EDITION.

Hours Before the Altar;
OR,
Meditations on the Holy Eucharist.

By Mgr. DE LA BOUILLERIE,
Coadjutor Bishop of Bordeaux.

*Translated and Enlarged from the Fifty-First French Edition.
By a Sister of Mercy.*

32mo, Cloth, - - 50 Cents.

These meditations which have passed through fifty-one editions in France are addressed to those pious souls who have tasted the sweetness of the Lord in the Sacrament of the Altar. They are published in the hope that they will suggest a method of meditating on the sweet mystery of the Most Blessed Sacrament, and that they may prove like those feeble lamps suspended before our Sanctuaries, which give light enough to guide our steps to the Tabernacle, but not enough to diminish the charm of its mysterious darkness, coming thus as an aid to prayer, but without taking from its recollection.

A Thought of St. Teresa's
FOR EVERY DAY IN THE YEAR.

Translated from the French by Miss ELLA McMAHON.

32mo, Extra Cloth, 50 Cents.

This little book contains the **most precious thoughts** of one of the greatest mystic writers of the Church.

In it the pious soul will find prayerful suggestions, food for meditation, and consoling words in time of affliction. Short and to the point, these **thoughts** will be recurred to daily, and it is hoped may soon become familiar to the lips of American Catholics.

BENZIGER BROTHERS, New York, Cincinnati, and Chicago.

The Centenary Edition.

VISITS TO THE
Most Holy Sacrament
AND TO
The Blessed Virgin Mary.

For Every Day in the Month.

By ST. ALPHONSUS DE LIGUORI,
Doctor of the Church.

EDITED BY
Rev. EUGENE GRIMM,
Priest of the Congregation of the Most Holy Redeemer.

32mo, cloth, - - - 50 cents.
" maroquette, - - 35 "

This **entirely new edition** of St. Alphonsus' admirable little work is printed from **new, large type,** and is the most easily read as well as the most beautiful edition ever issued. Besides the "Visits", it contains a number of Prayers with Devotions for Mass, and for Confession and Communion.

The "Visits to the Blessed Sacrament and to the Blessed Virgin" is the first work St. Alphonsus published, and was issued in the year 1745. From its first appearance it met with marvellous success not only in Italy, but in Europe and throughout the whole Catholic world. During the life of the saintly author it was translated into nearly every language, and now, after more than a century, the reputation that it has enjoyed, instead of diminishing, has ever increased.

BENZIGER BROTHERS, New York, Cincinnati, and Chicago.

Golden Sands.

FOURTH SERIES.

TRANSLATED FROM THE FRENCH
By Miss ELLA McMAHON.

32mo, Steel-plate Frontispiece, Cloth, 60 cts.

———o———

His Grace the Most Rev. Archbishop of Avignon, in approving this book, writes to the author: "It is a subject of rejoicing, and I am the first to rejoice at the appearance of the fourth series of your GOLDEN SANDS. The more we have of them the more we want; and as Our Lord has blessed the hunger and thirst after justice, it is fitting you should labor to gather, in even greater numbers, these fragments which I hope to see welded into precious ingots."

A THOUGHT FROM
Saint Francis of Assisi
AND HIS SAINTS
For Each Day of the Year.

TRANSLATED FROM THE FRENCH BY
MISS MARGARET A. COLTON.

32mo, Steel-plate Frontispiece, Cloth, 50 cts.

———o———

The voice of the Supreme Pontiff has so stirred the devotion of the faithful for the Seraph of Assisi and his "Army of Saints" that the publishers are encouraged to issue this little book in the hope that it will prove opportune and acceptable.

BENZIGER BROTHERS, New York, Cincinnati, and Chicago.

"We do not sufficiently remember our dead."
St. Francis de Sales.

A New Book by the Author of "Golden Sands."

Little Month of the Souls in Purgatory.

Translated from the French by

MISS ELLA McMAHON.

Supplemented by many Prayers for the Suffering Souls, A Rosary, A Way of the Cross, and A Manner of Hearing Mass for the Souls in Purgatory.

32mo, Black Maroquette, Silver Stamps on side, 35 cents.

This little book is a series of pious thoughts on our relations with the souls of our beloved dead.

By way of introduction will be found a brief exposition of the doctrine of the Catholic Church on the subject of Purgatory. On this doctrine is based every thought of the work, which therefore appeals more directly and confidently to the pious souls for whom it is specially written.

The author's aim is particularly **to console, to strengthen, and to lead to God souls cast down,** discouraged, and sometimes, alas! estranged from God by the death of loved ones,—souls of insufficient faith, unable to raise their eyes to heaven and behold those who have gone from them eternally happy with God, or awaiting a speedy entrance into eternal happiness. He seeks to soothe their grief, and help them to find again in spiritual intercourse with their dead that calmness and strength which enable us to endure life, to continue in the performance of our duty, and to fit ourselves to rejoin our loved ones in heaven, whither they are calling and awaiting us.

BENZIGER BROTHERS, New York, Cincinnati, and Chicago.

THE Truths of Salvation.

By Rev. J. PERGMAYR, S.J.

TRANSLATED FROM THE GERMAN BY A FATHER OF THE SAME SOCIETY. WITH THE PERMISSION OF SUPERIORS.

16mo, cloth. $1.00.

———o———

The basis of this work is "The Spiritual Exercises of St. Ignatius." The original is used as a book of Meditations, and also for retreats in nearly every Convent in Germany. Though written for those living in religious communities it will be found equally useful for Christians in the world, as it is offered to all who earnestly desire to consider the truths of salvation, and to acquire self-knowledge.

To those unaccustomed to meditate, or others who, from weakness or indisposition, are incapable of mental application, it will prove an efficient aid.

Solid Virtue:

A TRIDUUM AND SPIRITUAL CONFERENCES.

By Rev. Father BELLECIUS, S.J.

Translated from the original Latin, by a Father of the Society of Jesus. With the permission of Superiors.

16mo, cloth. 60 cents.

This is a translation of Fr. Bellecius's own abridgment of his larger work on Solid Virtue. It tells us in simplest language of all that goes to constitute genuine devotion, or solid virtue, how it may be practically acquired, what prevents many from attaining it, and how fruitful of choicest grace and happiness it is when attained. It is a book destined to advance numerous souls steadily on the path to Christian perfection, and generally to produce wide-spread and abiding good in the cloister, within the Sanctuary, and among lay Catholic people.

BENZIGER BROTHERS, New York, Cincinnati, and Chicago.

www.ingramcontent.com/pod-product-compliance
Lightning Source LLC
Chambersburg PA
CBHW020815230426
43666CB00007B/1028